ON THE
PATH
—— TO ——
JUSTICE

ON THE PATH TO JUSTICE

THE DANGEROUS MYTH OF EMPOWERMENT FOR WOMEN

LYNN BROMLEY

FREYDIS
ATHENEUM
South Portland, Maine

Copyright © 2022 Lynn Bromley

Published by Freydis Atheneum

All rights reserved. This book or parts thereof may not be reproduced in any form, stored in any retrieval system, or transmitted in any form by any means—electronic, mechanical, photocopy, recording, or otherwise—without prior written permission of the publisher, except as provided by United States of America copyright law. For information regarding permission requests, write to info@lynnbromley.com Attention: Permissions Coordinator.

ISBN 979-8-9853606-0-8   paperback

ISBN 979-8-9853606-1-5   ebook

Library of Congress Control Number 2021925145

First Edition

Book Publishing and Production by *Brands Through Books*.
www.brandsthroughbooks.com

By reading this document, the reader agrees that under no circumstances is the author or the publisher responsible for any losses, direct or indirect, which are incurred as a result of the use of information contained within this document, including, but not limited to, errors, omissions, or inaccuracies.

Legal Notice:

This book is copyright protected. Please note the information contained within this document is for educational and personal use only. You cannot amend, distribute, sell, use, quote, or paraphrase in writing any part, or the content within this book, without the consent of the author or publisher. The author invites you to quote her book in spoken words if you note the attribution.

info@lynnbromley.com

For my daughter, Claire, and our Foremothers

Amy Cox Bromley

Lucy Fletcher Cox

Gertrude Conger Bromley

and their Foremothers

and for every woman, our fellow travelers

on the path to justice

TABLE OF CONTENT

Introduction. "Extraordinary" Is a Setup — 1

Chapter 1. Women's Gifts, Women's Burdens — 5

Chapter 2. The Problem with Being Extraordinary — 11

Chapter 3. The Results of Systemic Gender Disparity — 27

Chapter 4. How We Work Against Ourselves — 53

Chapter 5. Reach Out, Not Up! — 67

Chapter 6. Fight Invisibility — 79

Chapter 7. The Magic of the Group Effect — 87

Chapter 8. Common Characteristics of Sister Groups — 101

Chapter 9. Commonly Held Goals — 111

Chapter 10. How to Build a Sister Group — 117

Chapter 11. Benefits of Sister Groups — 125

Chapter 12. No Matter What — 133

Acknowledgments — 141

About the Author — 145

Bibliography — 147

Privacy Statement

To respect the privacy of those friends and colleagues who may prefer not to be recognized, I have altered various personal details. To maintain confidentiality, I have changed names and other details that might identify certain individuals. If you recognize yourself in these pages, note that I have changed your name but kept your first initial.

Note to Readers

This publication contains the opinions and ideas of its author. It is intended to provide helpful and informative material on the subjects addressed. The strategies outlined in this book may not be suitable for every individual and are not guaranteed or warranted to provide any particular results.

No warranty is made with respect to the accuracy or completeness of the information referenced or contained herein, and both the author and the publisher specifically disclaim any responsibility for any liability, loss, or risk, personal or otherwise, which is incurred as a consequence, directly or indirectly, of the use and application of any of the contents of this book.

FROM THE AUTHOR

It is important to note that I did not invent the idea or practice of sisterhood. It is ancient and beautiful and has nourished individuals and cultures around the world for centuries. So, it is with palpable irony that many of the examples of sisterhood that have most inspired me—those I have admired for their strength, creativity, and results—are those I am the least acquainted with.

My dream for this book is that every woman can recognize herself and her sisters on some of the pages within. I apologize here to all those who cannot. Though I share the injustices that impact all women, by accident of birth and the privilege of safety and geography, there are depths to injustice that are beyond my experience and thus not fully acknowledged here. For those who may feel absent from these pages, please speak up. I so welcome your feedback on how to expand the relevance of these concepts to better include all women.

Here's to all the joy and discomfort in the boundary crossings ahead.

In sisterhood,
Lynn

INTRODUCTION

"Extraordinary" Is a Setup

I'M EXHAUSTED FROM DOING MY BEST AND NEAR BEST EVERY DAY. I AM afflicted with chronic extraordinary-ism, just like almost every woman I know.

There is a steady undercurrent of noise about how best to empower women, and how we can be empowered as women, while we continue to overfunction in a system that for generations has been rife with systemic gender inequality and oppression. We are deluged by an industry of self-improvement that seduces us with the promise of ease and happiness for the low cost of adopting an additional set of actions or attitudes. But individual improvement efforts do little to nothing to address the underlying issue that is the injustice of systemic gender inequity. Justice is nearer for us than it was for our foremothers, but we are not there yet.

So, what do we do in the meantime? We can't wait for justice. We live in the present and need and deserve to experience joy and abundance today. While on our way to justice, we must nourish ourselves and each other. We can do that by reaching toward each other, using the magic of sisterhood and the power of the group to remember and remind ourselves that women don't need to be empowered as much as we need to be unencumbered.

Recently, I was waiting for a friend in a Panera. Across the aisle from me was a man and his toddler. The toddler was doing what toddlers do, and the man was struggling to manage. I offered a bit of "we've all been there" humor, and a conversation followed. A few women stopped by to offer suggestions, admire the toddler, or to tell the stranger how nice it was to see a man out with his child.

The experience reminded me of a time twenty years before when I was standing in line with my toddler for a table at Friendly's. We were meeting my husband for lunch. I nervously wondered how much longer my toddler would tolerate standing in line as I watched several people be seated before we were. As I alerted the hostess to our spot in the line, she rolled her eyes and said, "Oh yeah." Shortly after, when my dressed-in-a-suit husband arrived, we were swiftly seated with smiles all around as the waitress said, "Meeting Daddy for lunch are you?"

Neither of these two seemingly similar scenarios looks dramatic on the surface, but the drama underneath is palpable for those of us who live in the isolation of invisibility in our everyday lives.

Being a woman in today's world, as it was in the worlds of our foremothers, is exhausting. Although each generation hands off its progress to the next—and we can certainly count gains and opportunities that our foremothers did not have—we are no less exhausted.

Why are we exhausted? Because we are encouraged to ignore generations of systemic inequality and oppression and act as if we are full and equal participants in society. Because we do this by chronically overfunctioning in order to fill in the gaps where the system fails us. Because we have bought into the premise we have been fed: that we can have it all—career, marriage, children, self-enlightenment—if we just become extraordinary. If we are just organized enough, positive enough, smart enough, and work hard enough.

But it is not true (yet). To thrive, we must see this idea for the lie it is. Only then can we see the truth. Only then can we see what needs to change and work toward it.

Such lies are the stuff that makes us buy the newest book on women's empowerment. The bookstores are full of them, as are my own shelves at home. They are the stuff that makes us grab another home organization magazine, thinking that if we just get our workspace and sleep space and kitchen up to standard, our lives will be easier. I laugh at my most recent decluttering effort, which included throwing out a dusty pile of organizing magazines I used for resting my coffee cup on. They are the stuff that makes us turn to fabulous weeknight meals in fifteen minutes with five ingredients. Yeah, that will help save time—until you have all the ingredients assembled and read two cups of *cooked* chicken as you look at the raw chicken in the package.

This is not a book about empowerment. Women have enough resilience and personal power and grit and gumption. We do not need to be told we can have it all if we just stand up straighter, speak more affirmatively, or lean in a bit more. That sort of "empowerment" puts it all on us to succeed in a system that is not rigged in our favor. It is a trap. We are not weak and in need of an infusion of power; we are simply overburdened and undernourished.

As one among you succeeding modestly while working mightily, as one among you tired of this advice, I write this book to suggest another way—one that is joyous, delightful, and effective. This book is in sacred recognition of my foremothers and all our foremothers, an homage to them for the ground they broke to get us here and a recognition of the debt we owe them to take it from here.

A Book for Our Daughters

I write this book for women and—perhaps more importantly—for my daughter and all our daughters, and for me, so I get to say this in the way I wish someone had said it to me.

I want to whisper in the ear of every woman who believes or feels that she is not working hard enough or smart enough or long enough or at the right things. I want to whisper, "*It's not you.*"

The system is against us. It relies on our competition with one another when what we ought to be doing is all those *other* C-words—connecting, communicating, cooperating, collaborating, and, yes, even conspiring and colluding on behalf of ourselves and our sisters when necessary, which is pretty much always.

It is time we drop the pretense that we can "have it all," particularly if we do not have childcare, or healthcare, or recognition for our work, or the opportunity to take a risk, or the ability to make a living wage, or the chance to get hired for our potential rather than for what we can prove we have done or know how to do.

There is no easy remedy for systemic injustice and long-established inequity. But we cannot wait for justice to thrive; we must nourish ourselves and each other along the path. As sisters, we can be careful to stand with, next to, and behind one another, and we must. This book is about how to do that.

This is not to say that the perspectives and suggested actions in this book won't benefit groups other than women. I would posit that they can, but I can only speak with authority, authenticity, and informed and relevant history as a woman experiencing gender-based injustice, observing the same in others, and engaging in the work of systemic change. All that is difficult enough, but with the addition of isolation and distance from one's sisters, it becomes soul-suckingly exhausting.

I write this book for all of us exhausted women so that we can better understand that *it is not us*. I want you to be able to say, "*No wonder!*" when you're halfway through and then discover a different way in the second half of the book.

A friend of mine, Mary, once said to me that she thought the most difficult thing about being a single mother was that there was no one to roll your eyes at when life was heavy or ridiculous. So, see me when I roll my eyes. Be my witness, and I will be yours, my sisters.

CHAPTER 1

WOMEN'S GIFTS, WOMEN'S BURDENS

Looking to the past is the first step to seeing the truth of our situation and knowing how to imagine and work for the future we want. So, to set our story in context, let me tell you the stories of my foremothers with the suspicion that they might resonate with yours.

The women in my line—in particular, my grandmothers, Nanny B. and Nan C., and my mother, Amy—were extraordinary. Against a swift and unrelenting current that had no interest in their success, they all succeeded beyond the expectations of their day.

My grandfathers were affable men whom people liked to hang out with. One was a wealthy businessman who played and drank too hard; the other, a funny, wise, and itinerant sawyer, carpenter, and farmhand who couldn't quite support his family. It was the grit and gumption of my grandmothers that handled what needed to get done. One grandmother was referred to by many as "a battle-ax"; the other, as someone who "didn't know how to loosen up and have fun."

Nanny B.: Gertrude

Nanny B., Gertrude, was a woman way ahead of her time. She was unusually challenged from her early days in school. She had had polio, and one leg was paralyzed, so she had to use a wheelchair. But the schools in the early 1900s were not set up for anything with wheels; there were stairs to manage just to get inside. Every day, her father would carry her and the chair up the steps, reversing the process at day's end. After three years of this, the school suggested that it was too difficult. And anyway, it was not as if she would ever use an education. Maybe it would be better if she didn't come back. So, at eleven years old, my grandmother was finished with her formal education.

As I recount this story, I remember her face as she told it to me—not for its sadness, but for its resignation. She eventually took correspondence courses from home and decided that she would learn bookkeeping. She told me that, no matter what, there would always be people in the world making money, and they would need someone to count it.

Nanny B. married my grandfather Bob in 1923 and enjoyed a very comfortable life. He was keen to provide all the needs of a modern household. He even bought my grandmother the first car in the state of Vermont with hand controls so she could have the independence of driving she had always dreamed of.

My grandfather was much-loved, handsome, charismatic, and a philanderer. When my grandmother discovered this, she embarked on a plan to divorce him and live on her own with her two children, a decision that was definitely not the norm in the 1940s.

She moved across the hall of their big house to a room of her own and set about finding a job. She visited many of the local businesses, who all refused to hire her, though several were looking for bookkeepers. She encountered all sorts of "reasons," such as "You don't have any experience," "We've never had a woman," and "What would Bob think?"

After weeks of disappointment, she revisited one business, as she had imagined a hesitation on the part of the owner before he dismissed her the first time. She decided she would make him an offer he couldn't refuse: to work for him for one year for no pay if he agreed to negotiate her worth to the company in good faith afterward. He took her up on her offer and "hired" her on immediately, adding a salary after six months, a feat my grandmother was proud of.

By the time she retired in 1967, she was the president of the company.

I've always had deep admiration for my Nanny B., but at the same time, I am saddened to understand the price she paid for her success in supporting her family. She had virtually no women friends, as being a "divorcée" carried a particular charge in those days. And I do not ever recall hearing her laugh. She would sometimes smile at something one of us did or said, but being carefree or doing something just for fun was not an experience she expected or sought.

I was in junior high, about fourteen, when my grandmother told me this story. I understood its import immediately, and I felt blessed to learn of it, as the other grandchildren knew only pieces of it. Thinking back, I know my grandmother needed to tell her story aloud, and I had somehow shown that I was the one to hear it.

NAN C.: LUCY

In the 1930s, Lucy's husband, my grandfather Harry, had a stroke that left him partially paralyzed on one side. Gradually he improved but walked with a prominent limp and did not regain much use of his dominant hand. Long before the days of disability insurance or welfare of any kind, the remedy for being indebted in New England was to be relegated to the town's "poor farms." These farms were usually ones that had been foreclosed upon for back taxes. The town would take them over and hire someone to manage the farm and care for the debtor residents, who were in those days called "inmates." My mother's family was clearly headed in that direction.

The 1930s were hard enough as it was, but with the addition of my grandfather's partial disability, the prospects for my mother's family of seven were grim. Yet, always practical, Lucy was reading the newspaper one day and noticed an article announcing the local poor farm needed an overseer. As my mother would often recount, Lucy turned and said to my grandfather, "Harry, since we're headed to the poor farm anyway, we might as well be running it."

That was the beginning of a period in my mother's life rich in lore, exploits, and life lessons, full of stories and memories she cherished. But the daily grind of making it all work fell, of course, to my grandmother. She ran the house—planning the meals, assembling and supervising the kitchen crew, doing the laundry, and housecleaning. My grandfather was "in charge" of the farm chores—milking, haying, planting, and harvesting—but this amounted to him telling my grandmother what needed to be done so she could assign the work to the hands. He said she was a better manager, but, in reality, my grandfather just preferred to be the nice guy.

Later in life, in her mid-sixties, when one should be thinking about retirement, my grandmother still needed to work for pay. None of the years of work she had done at the poor farm counted in any calculation of retirement income. So, when the poor farm was closed, and after a brief period of running a local boardinghouse, my grandmother moved to a state-run children's home as the live-in manager, getting special permission from the governing board for my grandfather to live there, as she was his major financial support. As unusual as this was at the time, it was never a topic for discussion—except for my mother explaining that it would be embarrassing for my grandfather if anyone mentioned it.

My Grandmothers' Gifts to Me

Hearing about my grandmothers' successes doing things that were extraordinary—things that women did not typically do, with no support and to general scorn—alongside my ne'er-do-well grandfathers gave me my first real dose of what gender-based unfairness looked like. That experience created in me a lifelong tendency to catch unfairness. At times, this awareness of injustice immobilized me. At others, it lit my sense of justice to fuel all sorts of activism, protests, and advocacy—some momentary, some sustainable, some exhilarating, and some frustrating.

I thank my grandmothers for passing along their grit and gumption, but I know that they would not want to pass along the sense of invisibility, isolation, and exhaustion that came with their daily grind to be extraordinary. My grandmothers broke ground by doing things that were not considered "women's work." When they did so without complaint, the system did not get the cue that one of the parts of the economic machine was overworking and would likely tire or fail. When we work hard, longing to be extraordinary, we tire. The effort is unsustainable, and we become the brittle link in the system.

Our foremothers picked up their burdens and moved on. Their gift to us is greater awareness and greater choice. Now, our job is to take our mothers' and grandmothers' work to the next level: We need to show the system that we are exhausted and in need of attention. As we work for justice, we must begin with one another. We must redefine thriving as something that includes joy and ease and agree about what we will pass on to our daughters' generation. But first, let's look at the status quo we live in—and the lie we have all swallowed.

Chapter 2

The Problem with Being Extraordinary

Take these words and imagine using them to describe something: *usual, normal, standard, typical, stock, common, customary, habitual, accustomed, wonted, regular, routine, day-to-day, settled, traditional.* Imagine a normal day, or a standard meal, or a common job. Do you feel their neutrality? Their negativity?

These are all synonyms for *ordinary*. I suspect that most of us, like my foremothers, have long abandoned ordinary and adopted a daily pursuit of *extra*ordinary. Extraordinary is beyond ordinary. It is *remarkable, exceptional, preeminent*. How many of us aspire to be this every day? Imagine interviewing someone for a position, and as you detail the job description, you add that the applicant is expected to be *remarkable, exceptional, amazing, astonishing, astounding, marvelous, wonderful, sensational, stunning, incredible, unbelievable*, or even *miraculous*. It is an outrageous expectation, yet it is what we expect of ourselves and each other—other *women*, that is.

There seems to be a sad commonality that unites all women: fatigue. And for most of us, exhaustion. Many of us think of this as just the way it is: There is much to be done, and we are the ones to do it, so on with it we get. When we deconstruct the days of many women, they have that "how in the hell did she do all that?" sort of character. I know many of mine do, and my daughter's, and . . . well, let me just say, every woman I know.

For most of my thirty-plus-year career, I have watched the injustice that women suffer, largely silently, every day. Though this disquieting perspective is not always pleasant, I thank my grandmothers for equipping me with it.

Much like my grandmothers, perhaps, women have bought into the myth that if we work harder, faster, and smarter to be more organized, more creative, and more original, we will speed up our ease and success. If we strive to be extraordinary every day, eventually we will be able to rest.

This way of being is exhausting. I can feel the weariness as I describe this reality and think back on all the times I went above and beyond with great effort only to receive no particular reward. It is important to understand that being chronically extraordinary is not in our best interests, nor in the interests of women as a whole.

Our exhaustion breeds frustration as a daily experience. We constantly juggle dynamic priorities of our own and of those around us—kids are sick, assistant did not come in, colleague's family is facing a crisis, there is a toilet paper shortage—with that "somebody's got to do it" resignation.

Our frustration breeds overwhelm because we know, on some level, that this is not a pace we can keep up forever. When we begin to be enlightened, we realize this is not a pace we even *want* to keep up for much longer. Enter the books and magazines and courses and yoga and mindfulness training professing to make us better at being extraordinary.

These false starts and remedies breed negative self-talk—the impolite and unintelligent questions we ask ourselves and statements we say to ourselves: "What am I doing wrong here?" "I need to X more or Y less or buy a Z." "What do I need to do to be as good as _____?"

One of the tragic results of all of this fatigue and overwhelm is the resentment that we start to feel and how that serves to separate us from our sisters.

Women's empowerment is a false promise. But more than that, it is a dangerous myth because individual behaviors will not change a system that stands against women's success. We don't need to be empowered. We need to be unencumbered from generations of injustice and unachievable expectations.

THE SYSTEMIC NATURE OF THE PROBLEM

My grandmothers' stories first brought the problem of gender inequity to my attention. But it starts way before that, in infancy, in subtle and not-so-subtle ways. It begins with expectations of what we will and will not do, which shapes the norms of our future. With what we can and can't do without challenging a norm.

I will share the stories of my family's and my own journey, and as you read, I invite you to consider what your experience and your foremothers' experiences of gender inequity have been in the workforce.

DIVISION OF LABOR—BOY JOBS AND GIRL JOBS

We learn at an early age that there are jobs we are expected to do and jobs we are not expected to do. I grew up near my uncle's farm and spent a lot of time there with my cousin Billy. There was always something that needed doing at the farm, especially during haying season. On one such busy day, the hay in the lower field needed to be raked. Billy and I headed there. I stationed myself in the shade at the edge of the field, sitting among the rocks of the old tumbled-down wall. I had a thermos of cool water and a stack of Billy's Marvel comic books (mostly *Superman*) to keep me occupied while he raked. He got to drive the team of horses ahead of the dump rake, and I got to sit by the creek.

I had fled the house chores, wishing I could drive the team. Jim and Dan were big and gentle old horses; even if they started to run, they would quickly return to plodding. I knew I could handle them, but no one would let me, partly because we had just moved to town and didn't farm, but mostly because I was a girl. Even then, they did not say it—but I knew.

The jobs on the farm were divided into two groups: boy jobs and girl jobs. Boy jobs were fun. They did something or made something and were a little dangerous and thus exciting. Girl jobs were, well, mostly about feeding and taking care of the family and the workers, minding the kitchen garden, canning things, and cleaning. In other words, cleaning up after the men. My aunt would feed the calves that arrived in the spring, but the birthing of the calves was men's work. When Bessy (they called them all Bessy) started to moo very loudly and dance back and forth, the women were sent up to the house. Really.

My mother had very cleverly managed to escape from kitchen duty, as she called it. I asked her once how it was that she got to do the many "boy" jobs that I had heard her talk about. She simply said, "I failed so miserably at all the kitchen stuff that Mama finally just said, 'Go ahead down to the barn and help your father.'"

I am not sure my mother recognized this for the brilliant strategy that it was. No arguing about how much she preferred barn chores to house chores. No discussion about what she was best at doing—just her silent protest against the kitchen work and her acquiescence to what was expected of her.

Challenging the Norm of Boy Jobs and Girl Jobs

The world of work beyond the farm was also made up of girl jobs and boy jobs. This gender-based division of labor was established long ago, and though we may think of it as a construct of the past, it is not.

My mother was a schoolteacher for her entire career. She began just after college in the late 1940s, teaching eight grades in a one-room schoolhouse, where she had to arrive early enough to light the boiler. She boarded with a local family and had a curfew, as teachers had to model firm moral guidelines for their students.

After the war, as men returned home and reentered the workforce, they also flocked to the teaching profession in greater numbers. They were routinely paid more than even the veteran women teachers and soon started to supplant the women—particularly the married ones, since their husbands could support them. My mother told me she wore her wedding band on a chain around her neck so no one would know she was married and did not confess the truth until she was pregnant with me and had to resign.

My generation grew up with a very clear family model. Dads went to work, and moms took care of the house and the kids. Most families were one-income families. Growing up in a close-knit, post-war housing development in Vermont gave me a nearly idyllic childhood. The dads were away during the day, and most of the moms stayed home. Actually, *all* the moms in my neighborhood stayed home—except mine, who returned to teaching when my younger sister started kindergarten.

We were an oddity. I felt a bit uncomfortable that we rarely had homemade cookies to share and that our meals were uninspiring. My mother didn't know how to fix my sister's or my hair with barrettes or braids, and when she decided to sew matching dresses for us, the material lay on the sewing machine pinned to thin brown paper and never got finished. And, of course, I couldn't ever have anyone over after school because my mother wasn't home in the afternoons. All of this left me in a perpetual state of disappointment and even more than that—embarrassment that my mother did not measure up to the neighborhood standard.

Still, the rhythm of our days was easy and predictable: We began with breakfast prepared by our mothers, went off to school, then came home to play outside until we were called in to a supper also prepared by our mothers, then watched TV while our mothers did the dishes (and we girls helped) until bedtime, when we were tucked in by our mothers—which was when mine did the laundry. I do not recall wondering why my dad was not doing house chores, but I do remember thinking how lucky the other moms were that they had all day to relax while we were at school and our fathers at work. That was the norm then. Now, some fifty years later, not enough has changed to accommodate the lives of women needing to work for pay.

When my mother went back to teaching, it was a financial necessity, as my father was a sparse and spotty "provider." But, again, he was shielded from the general public knowing that because of my mother's financial contribution to the family, while she suffered the scorn of many in our neighborhood. Somewhat ironically, had that not been the case, I know my mother would have preferred working for pay to homemaking.

Just as my mother had fled the "girl chores" of the house and worked when her peers did not, so too did I flee the girl jobs expected of my generation. My father lovingly told me I should be a nurse or a teacher so that wherever my husband might have to go, I could always find a job there. I did not want to be either, but I did not know how to begin imagining what else I could do, what I might be good at, or what I would love. So, I became a teacher and then quit before I really got started. After that, I worked in a truck repair garage and an auto parts store, and I drove tractor trailers cross-country with my then-boyfriend.

When I finally settled down to find a "real" job, I worked for a prominent grocery chain, where I eventually became only the second woman promoted to a management position. At my first management meeting in the executive conference room with the guys sitting around in the big chairs, my feet didn't touch the floor.

INEQUITY IN THE WORK WORLD TODAY

There are myriad studies, articles, and documentaries on gender inequality in the workplace, but I will quickly list the main characters in this very old story:

Unequal Pay – In the United States today, a slim majority (50.8%) of the population is female.[1] Additionally, women are more educated than men and have been since 1982. To be more specific, "Women have earned more bachelor's degrees than men since 1982, more master's degrees than men since 1987, and more doctorate degrees than men since 2006."[2]

---

1 "Census 2020 Quick Facts," United States Census Bureau, April 1, 2020, www.census.gov/quickfacts/fact/table/US/SEX255219#SEX255219.

2 "Women in the Workforce: United States (Quick Take)," Catalyst, October 14, 2020, www.catalyst.org/research/women-in-the-workforce-united-states/;

And yet, women's pay is nowhere near equitable in comparison with men's pay. Though most studies note that, on average, women earn $0.80 to men's $1.00 (and even lower for women of color), a 2018 study stated that it is much closer to $0.49 and $1.00 when adding in part-time work, which is overwhelmingly performed by women—many of whom are also raising children.[3]

Unequally Promoted – Despite the numbers regarding population and education, women make up just 5% of CEOs in the US. There are fewer than 10% women in Standard and Poor's top-earner category.[4]

Sexual Harassment – A 2019 survey found that 38% of women said they have been sexually harassed at work, and a subset of women—tipped workers and those lacking legal immigration status—are twice as likely to experience sexual harassment at work.[5] Looking deeper into the detail, we can see that sexual harassment of women is an intrinsic part of today's workplace:[6]

- 63% of victims do not file a complaint;
- 72% of victims were harassed by someone more senior in their workplace;

Richard V. Reeves and Ember Smith, "The Male College Crisis Is Not Just in Enrollment, But Completion," Brookings, October 8, 2021, www.brookings.edu/blog/up-front/2021/10/08/the-male-college-crisis-is-not-just-in-enrollment-but-completion/.

3 Emily Peck, "The Gender Wage Gap Is Even Worse Than You Thought," HuffPost, November 28, 2018, www.huffpost.com/entry/gender-wage-gap_n_5bfd9d3fe4b0771fb6befd55.

4 "Historical Women CEOs of the Fortune Lists: 1972-2021 (List)," Catalyst, June 4, 2021, www.catalyst.org/research/historical-list-of-women-ceos-of-the-fortune-lists-1972-2021/.

5 Minda Zetlin, "54 Percent of Women Report Workplace Harassment. How Is Your Company Responding?," Inc., March 2018, www.inc.com/magazine/201804/minda-zetlin/sexual-harassment-workplace-policy-metoo.html.

6 Alexis Best, "16 Alarming Sexual Harassment in the Workplace Statistics You Need to Know," Inspired eLearning, July 12, 2021, inspiredelearning.com/blog/sexual-harassment-in-the-workplace-statistics/.

- 55% of victims experience retaliation after speaking up or making a claim; and,
- according to victims who have reported harassment, 95% of the men go unpunished.

Inequality in Starting Pay – New research from Glassdoor found that women negotiated their salary much less often than men. The poll found that 70% of women accepted the salary they were offered, while only 52% of men did the same.[7]

Beyond paid work, the work of women providing care for children or others is completely invisible. Caregiving, although a basic necessity, is not counted in GDP calculations and thus not taken into account in most legislative and policy discussions.

Meg Conley, a young woman who gives brilliant, simple messages via her blog, *homeculture*, Instagram, and newsletters, has chosen to make homemaking her primary activity.[8] She is what we too often refer to as a "stay-at-home mom." This is clearly her choice, but it is not a choice without cost, as she carefully outlines.

We give lots of lip service to the value of caregiving and homemaking, but that value is not something that supports women. It is not something that women can spend or invest. Breadwinning is much more highly valued than caregiving, so breadwinners make the majority of the family financial decisions, although it is the caregivers who keep the systems running.

Conley describes her already difficult two-parent, middle-class experience of managing a home, school, and children during the 2020 pandemic and helps us to better imagine the life of a working single mom who has no respite, who cannot afford time off, and who must choose to slide deeper into poverty or leave her seven-year-old at home alone to do remote learning while she works.

---

7   "3 in 5 Employees Did Not Negotiate Salary," Glassdoor, last modified August 2, 2020, www.glassdoor.com/blog/3-5-u-s-employees-negotiate-salary/.

8   You can find her work @_megconley.

Rather than paraphrase Conley's brilliant insights, I will simply quote her here, where she draws our attention to the nearly completely ignored reality: Stay-at-home moms are in charge of the success ecosystem.

> "[E]very broken institution depends on the unpaid labor of caretakers, and those caretakers are cracking and near broken themselves. America's dismissive attitude toward care work disproportionately hurts our most exploited community builders: Black women and women of color. They are hurt when they engage in professional work as underpaid caretakers who cannot afford childcare for their own children. They are hurt when their home-based care work builds our communities, and we consume their labor without pay. We must stop solely thinking about the best way to help mothers lean in and start diversifying the way we compensate them as community builders.
>
> "Motherhood in America is a scam. We're told if we work hard enough, raise our children well, and faithfully support the American dream, then we'll end up on top. No one ever mentions how the hierarchy of success is shaped like a pyramid. A few mothers get to the top. They give TED Talks and write self-help books. But mostly, we're the cracking base of a condemned structure. America has never really cared about mothers. If I wasn't certain of this before, 2020 has made it abundantly clear. The pandemic hit mothers the hardest, yet no one came to help us. Instead, we've been asked to dig deeper, push ourselves, and invest more of ourselves in this 'once in a lifetime opportunity.'"[9]

---

[9] Meg Conley, "Motherhood in America Is a Multilevel Marketing Scheme," Medium, December 7, 2020, gen.medium.com/motherhood-in-america-is-a-multilevel-marketing-scheme-f4ec1f536b04.

Impact of the COVID-19 Pandemic on Women

Not that we need a study to confirm what we know in our experience and observations, but seeing it in study after study helps us to realize *no wonder* we are exhausted, dispirited, and hitting a wall.

According to McKinsey's "Women in the Workplace 2021" study, women are more vulnerable to COVID-19-related economic effects because of existing gender inequalities that have been made worse by the impacts of the pandemic.[10]

Women are even more burned out now than they were a year ago, and the gap between women and men has almost doubled. In the past year, one in three women has considered leaving the workforce or downshifting her career—a significant increase from the previous one in four studied during the first few months of the pandemic.[11]

To begin with, women's jobs are 1.8 times more vulnerable to this crisis than men's jobs, since women are disproportionately represented in service sector jobs such as hospitality and retail.[12] Pre-pandemic, women already performed an average of 75% of the world's unpaid care work such as childcare, care for the elderly, and cooking and cleaning, and that burden has increased significantly during COVID-19.[13] McKinsey's *Power of Parity* research found that women in the United States added 1.52 additional hours of unpaid labor each day during the pandemic.[14] Add to that the immense and dynamic demands on teachers and healthcare workers, who are also predominantly women, and it is no wonder that "women

---

10 "Women in the Workplace 2021," McKinsey & Company, September 27, 2021, www.mckinsey.com/featured-insights/diversity-and-inclusion/women-in-the-workplace.

11 "Women in the Workplace 2021."

12 Anu Madgavkar et al., "COVID-19 and Gender Equality: Countering the Regressive Effects," McKinsey Global Institute, July 15, 2020, www.mckinsey.com/featured-insights/future-of-work/covid-19-and-gender-equality-countering-the-regressive-effects.

13 "COVID-19 and Gender Equality."

14 "COVID-19 and Gender Equality."

have dropped out of the workforce at a higher rate than explained by labor-market dynamics alone."[15]

WAGE DEFLATION

In addition to the division of labor, we have wage deflation, which simply means that wages do not keep pace with inflation. In 1980, the federal minimum wage was $3.10. In 2009, it was raised to $7.25, where it has remained until 2021. Though several states have since mandated higher minimums, those increases have not been enough.[16]

Well into my high school years and beyond, single-income families were the norm. If partnered women, like my mother, were in the workforce, it was often their choice. It was not impossible to raise a family on one income. Today, having only one income would be unusual even for middle- to high-income families, never mind those in entry-level or part-time work. Most women do not have the choice to stay home and depend on a partner's single income.

One of my high school friends, Betty, got pregnant and had to leave school in our senior year ("had to"—a story for another time). Her boyfriend and later-husband, Bill, deferred college and kept working so that he and Betty could have their own apartment and she could stay home with the baby. He pumped gas at our local hardware-and-everything-else store and eventually became the assistant manager. They were able to live comfortably enough to eat, pay rent, buy a car, and pay their bills.

Contrast that with the economics of 2021 when the average salary for a convenience store assistant manager is $33,000 a year, or $17.00 an hour,

---

15 "COVID-19 and Gender Equality."

16 "State Minimum Wage Laws," U.S. Department of Labor, last modified September 30, 2021, www.dol.gov/agencies/whd/minimum-wage/state; David Cooper, Zane Mokhiber, and Ben Zipperer, "Raising the Federal Minimum Wage to $15 by 2025 Would Lift the Pay of 32 Million Workers: A Demographic Breakdown of Affected Workers and the Impact on Poverty, Wages, and Inequality," Economic Policy Institute, March 9, 2021, www.epi.org/publication/raising-the-federal-minimum-wage-to-15-by-2025-would-lift-the-pay-of-32-million-workers.

well above minimum wage but far from enough to cover the cost of living for a family of three. The average rent for a two-bedroom apartment in the US is $1,964 a month, with much higher rates in and around urban areas, averaging from $3,000 in Midwestern cities to $5,000-$6,000 in East Coast cities.[17]

As Emmie Martin of CNBC writes: "These days, in no state does working 40 hours a week for minimum wage enable a person to rent a median two-bedroom apartment, let alone begin to build wealth for the future."[18]

Plainly said, many women go to work while piecing together expensive and difficult-to-find childcare because they must, not because they choose to.

Women's Labor as a Commodity

Though women represent more than 50% of the population and are more likely than not to be working for pay outside their home, despite numerous policy attempts, the workplace is not much more welcoming to women today than it was fifty years ago.

Women's labor operates as a commodity in the United States economy. In World War II, when so many men were away, women were invited into the workforce, trained for whatever jobs needed to be done, paid well, and applauded for their contribution to the war effort.

The now-iconic poster of Rosie the Riveter was part of a national campaign to encourage women to do "boy jobs." And women entered the workforce in large numbers, enjoying the work, the pay, and the status of being mission-critical to our economy.

The obvious problem of what to do with the children was addressed by a comprehensive federal effort to build childcare facilities, training and

---

17 "Rent Report, October 2021: The State of the Rental Market," Apartment Guide, October 29, 2021, www.apartmentguide.com/blog/rent-report-october-2021-the-state-of-the-rental-market/.

18 Emmie Martin, "Here's How Much More Expensive Life Is for You Than It Was for Your Parents," CNBC, June 21, 2017, www.cnbc.com/2017/06/21/life-is-much-more-expensive-for-you-than-it-was-for-your-parents.html.

staffing them and subsidizing the cost. Yes, seventy-seven years ago, the United States had *federally subsidized quality childcare* at a cost of $0.50 a day (equivalent to $7.52 today) per child.[19] When the war was over and the men returned, the childcare centers were closed almost immediately.[20]

I heard about this little-known part of our history firsthand from some of the women who had been recruited to work at "boy jobs" on behalf of the war effort. I was the gender equity coordinator at the local technical college, and for the college's fiftieth anniversary in 1997, I was tasked with developing some programming for Women's History Month. I discovered a handful of nearby women who had actually worked in one of the two wartime shipyards formerly located near the current location of the campus. Women shipbuilders. Women who had built Liberty ships in the 1940s.

I assembled several of the women for an interview that was filmed by the video production class. The content was so compelling that I raised the money to produce a broadcast-quality version. The film was called *On the Job: Women Launching a New Tradition*. This was a bit of a play on words, as hands-on technical education and training was still, in the 1990s, referred to as "nontraditional" training for women.

The women's voices were strong and their faces brilliant as they shared their stories.

- Helen: "I had five children, and it was dangerous work at the yard. I was often afraid, but I always felt lucky to be making all that money. Every day, I'd stop just before entering the yard and say a little prayer that I'd get to go home OK that day. People got hurt."

- Marion: "I was a burner. It was rough work and I loved it. I would cut the steel with a torch. It was a bit like laying out a dress pattern,

---

19 "CPI Inflation Calculator," U.S. Bureau of Labor Statistics, accessed December 13, 2021, www.bls.gov/data/inflation_calculator.htm.

20 Rafael Nam, "'I Come Up Short Every Day': Couples Under Strain As Families Are Stuck At Home," NPR, November 12, 2020, www.npr.org/2020/11/12/929551120/i-come-up-short-every-day-couples-under-strain-as-pandemic-upends-life-at-home.

but instead of cutting the cloth with scissors, I was cutting the steel with a torch."

- Shirley: "I was a Heliarc welder, and a good one. There were only a few of us who could weld on this certain part of the ship. A good weld would look like a stack of quarters lying on its side, and you could run your hand along it and the slag would just snap right off, leaving it gleaming and beautiful. I'd like to strike an arc one more time before I die."

I also asked the women about what happened after the war.

- Helen: "I went back to taking care of my children and to regular work. Never made that much money again. It was hard."

- Shirley: "Boy, I hated to leave. I worked in the school cafeteria after that so I could be home when the kids got out of school."

- Marion: "I don't know what to say about this. The boys were coming home, and they needed jobs, so we had to step aside. We didn't really think it was strange back then. But I couldn't find any work that I didn't dislike—until I started making jewelry. Later I taught at the art school. I was lucky to find something I loved. I was still working with metal—just making a necklace instead of building a ship."[21]

Women Are Guests in Our Economy

Women's labor has long served as a safety valve in our economy. When jobs are plentiful and workers hard to find, we are welcomed into the workforce. When the economy contracts or there are mass layoffs (as in the 2020 pandemic), we are not quite so welcomed. Women shipbuilders were recruited, admired, paid well, and applauded. After the war, they were excused to their former lives. The daycare centers were dismantled, and they became a part of history instead of a story of progress.

---

21 The film can be watched in its entirety here: archive.org/details/OnTheJobWomenLaunchingANewTradition.

Although I do not deny the progress we have made, I do assert that it has been much too slow, modest at best, as evidenced by the gender disparity and pain experienced as a result of the pandemic's economic contraction. The service economy, where women make up the vast majority of workers, was hardest hit. In particular, the hospitality subset was decimated while Congress debated whether a one-time payment of $1,400 was too much and if an additional $600 unemployment benefit check would encourage people to stay home instead of finding a job.

Sadly, our economy depends on low-wage work, and women disproportionately hold these jobs. When jobs are scarce, the systemic forces of an economy based overwhelmingly on profit rather than values are happy to excuse them. The workplace expects us to come as well-behaved guests, act accordingly, and know when to leave. It does not expect us to move in and thus has made no permanent accommodations for us. Chairs that are too big, women's bathrooms inconveniently located, no provisions for childcare or healthcare, no cogent policies on childbearing and rearing—the workplace is still a foreign country for women. And just like operating in any foreign country, it is exhausting to figure out the code, find the workarounds, and manage being ignored or rejected. It is clear that it is up to us to find a solution.

FORTUNATELY, WE ARE NOT ALWAYS WELL-BEHAVED GUESTS

During filming, Marion impishly told us a story of "stowing away" on a ship as it launched for its shakedown cruise. She explained that women were not allowed aboard when a ship was underway. It was an old tradition, she noted: "We were supposed to be bad luck or something like that."

She told one of the seamen how much she wanted to go for the ride, and he helped her with an ingenious plot. There were two ways to enter the ship when it was being built: up the gangway or by climbing the pipes to the scaffolding.

"I was very good at climbing the pipes," she said. "I was fast."

He coached her on how to wait until the ship was just about to launch and then climb up the pipes and hop aboard. She did just that to cheers on the part of her sister shipbuilders and some of the seamen, as well as to a chorus of "Hey, you can't do that! Come back here, you'll be arrested!" from the bosses.

She spoke inspiringly about how it felt to look back at the shipyard from the bay and how much she enjoyed walking around the boat that she had helped to build and that was overwhelmingly made by women's labor. As they turned back toward shore, she began to worry about being caught and arrested. But her co-conspirator said, "Don't you worry, come with me."

He took her into the galley and helped her climb into one of the giant ovens. He said, "They'll never find you here. Just stay here until you're sure they've gone. You'll be fine."

She giggled as she told us about rolling to the back of the oven and waiting until near dark to come out.

Marion was not a well-behaved guest. She didn't change history with that single act, but taking that forbidden ride on behalf of her sister shipbuilders nudged it a bit off its course.

Perhaps you have recognized yourself in these pages and how the myth of empowerment has operated in your life and resulted in your experience of systemic injustice for women. Have you been a well-behaved guest? We have come far beyond boy jobs and girl jobs but not as far as we had hoped, as we will see next.

CHAPTER 3

THE RESULTS OF SYSTEMIC GENDER DISPARITY: THE NEED TO BE EXTRAORDINARY

Every one of the women I have highlighted so far was extraordinary. Each made a way for herself and her family not because of, but in spite of, societal norms. Every woman reading this book can recognize how often she acts extraordinarily—often for quite ordinary results—sometimes by choice, but mostly by necessity. Walking uphill, swimming against the tide, carrying others' burdens—pick your favorite metaphor, but consider the cost of accepting chronic overwork as the norm.

My foremothers had little choice, just as many of us are not blessed with the luxury of choice, but as long as chronic overwork (including misplaced self-improvement) is a cost that we are willing to pay, it is unlikely to change.

CHRONIC EXTRAORDINARY-ISM

When I first began speaking about this problem, I posed the question, "What if we just started doing the minimum instead of the maximum? What if we were visibly ordinary instead of invisibly extraordinary?"

Ordinary has a negative connotation. But what if ordinary was *enough* for most days? Then, when we, on occasion, delivered extraordinary work, it might be noted, appreciated, or even rewarded.

I was met with lots of pushback from some of my most admired friends and colleagues. The words would differ, but the message was the same: "So, what, we just start doing incomplete, sloppy work?"

It is a valid question. How do we reboot the world to expect less than extraordinary performance from women?

As we talked about turning from *extraordinary* and embracing simply *ordinary*, a discussion of men's mediocre performance invariably ensued. This included quite specific descriptions of men being recognized and promoted for unremarkable performance when it would not be the case for women.

In every one of these conversations, across age and geography and socioeconomic status, the goal was always the same: to somehow get women's work recognized for not being simply equal to our male counterparts' work but, very often, superior. A 2020 study by Goldman Sachs found that "companies with more women in management and board positions outperformed their male-led counterparts."[22] Articles have been written about it, and we have statistics and studies to prove it: Women's performance is equal to or exceeds that of men's. This is a frustrating and dispiriting reality.

As I was doing research for this book, my Google and Amazon algorithm was re-calibrated so that it offered me interesting books based on what I was searching. One of the offerings that amused me was the book *Why Do So Many Incompetent Men Become Leaders?* by Tomas Chamorro-Premuzic. Instead of asking this question, we should think about trading in our daily pursuit of extraordinary to instead lean into the same sort of "incompetence" that elevates men to positions of leadership.

I once heard someone say, "We will know we have reached gender equity when mediocre women can reach the heights of mediocre men."

---

22 Emily Graffeo, "Companies with More Women in Management Have Outperformed Their More Male-Led Peers, According to Goldman Sachs," Markets Business Insider, November 11, 2020, markets.businessinsider.com/news/stocks/companies-women-management-leadership-stock-market-outpeformance-goldman-sachs-female-2020-11.

The response was a laugh and an eye roll. But in none of the conversations I have had with other women has there been any serious thought or words put to the idea of doing less, doing enough, or doing something ordinary to even the proverbial playing field.

But how about it? How about a cure for chronic extraordinary-ism?

THE E-CYCLE™: THE HAMSTER WHEEL WE'RE ON

Before we find the cure, we must see the hamster wheel we spin in and are spun in.

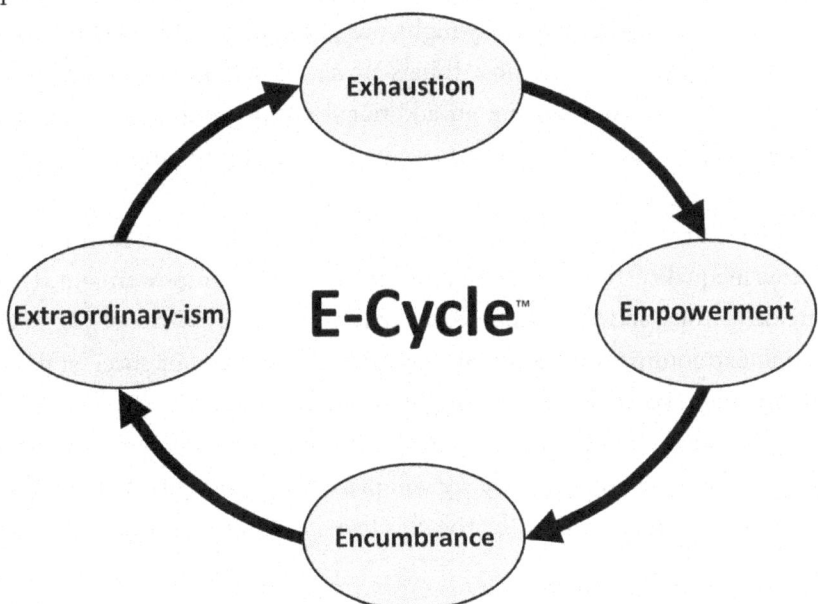

As you look at this cycle, imagine where you are on it at this very moment. You begin by being *extraordinary* in order to be appropriately recognized or valued. You do the assigned task and a little more—you make a clever and original Halloween costume, or you perform an emergency DIY repair of the leak under the sink—and now the bar is set for you to do these things again and again.

Now the daily expectation of more and better begins to lead to *exhaustion*. It is here that we are faced with the choice of doing less or maintaining our current above-average performance. This does not present itself as one decision, as it often becomes a way of life before we realize the cycle we are in.

Enter the purported solution of *empowerment*. We are enticed and offered a myriad of courses, books, articles, gadgets, schedules, and more to ostensibly reduce the need to be extraordinary, or at least to make extraordinary performance easier. The myth of empowerment is that a set of individual behaviors can move us out of this cycle. If we lean in, stand up straight, speak more clearly, negotiate better, wash our faces, and get our meal prepping done on Sunday night, our problems will be solved. That is the tacit promise. But all those things are simply additions to our already too long to-do list. They are an additional encumbrance to our already oversized share of the burden. Ah, we have just added yet another E-word to the cycle: *encumbrance*.

Any set of individual behaviors is far from sufficient to solve systemic inequality. These pseudo-solutions are pseudo-empowerment. They are dangerous, and they support the myth that we can solve our plight by being extraordinary in new ways every day. If we are not successful, we only need to buy a new book, gadget, or . . .

This fork in the path is where someone ought to place a giant BEWARE sign. This is where *we* will place such a sign because we need to see ourselves and each other on this hamster wheel before we can slow it down and get off.

It Is Not the Pipeline

For every study that shows women succeeding in categories formerly dominated by men, there are many more studies that show precious little progress in real terms. The number of women entering graduate school, medical and law schools, STEM (science, technology, engineering, and math) fields, and getting PhDs has vastly improved in recent decades. "In 1970, women made up 38% of all U.S. workers and 8% of STEM workers. By 2019, the STEM proportion had increased to 27% with women making up 48% of all workers."[23] The STEM pipeline has a steady flow of more women than in decades past, and this "pipeline" issue is considered solved in many institutions and programs in higher education.

But the pipeline leaks. Just look a few years after graduation and notice the significant drop in women who make it or manage to stay on the progress-and-promotion or entrepreneur path in their chosen profession. Well-prepared, well-educated, competent women are leaking across the landscape due to a lack of willingness or ability to meet the market—and sadly, their own—expectations of consistently delivering on the promise of being extraordinary in order to earn their place in the higher wage job market. The women who remain do so at great cost.

The 2020 Goldman Sachs study on the superior performance of women-led companies noted that "in a basket of 600 European stocks, companies with more female leadership saw their share price outperform on average by 2.5% a year compared with companies with less women leaders."[24] Yet, in 2017, women-only founding teams accounted for only 2.2% of total venture capital funding. In comparison, 79% of total venture capital funding was raised by men-only teams.[25] No wonder women are burning out.

This surprising-to-some phenomenon is now referred to as the "leaky pipeline." There is no shortage of opinion about why it is that the pipeline, now more adequately filled on the front end, is failing to deliver much output. It is another consequence of the subtle yet powerful systemic oppression women face. It may also be related to our next (unsubtle) topic: unpaid labor.

---

23 Anthony Martinez and Cheridan Christnacht, "Women Are Nearly Half of U.S. Workforce but Only 27% of STEM Workers," United States Census Bureau, January 26, 2021, www.census.gov/library/stories/2021/01/women-making-gains-in-stem-occupations-but-still-underrepresented.html.

24 Graffeo, "Companies with More Women in Management."

25 "35 Women-Owned Business Statistics You Need to Know in 2021," Great Business Schools, last modified May 18, 2021, www.greatbusinessschools.org/women-owned-business-statistics/.

THE ADDITIONAL BURDEN OF UNPAID LABOR

When the forty-hour workweek became the norm, a family typically included a man working and a woman at home. The man worked for pay, and the woman worked to keep the home and mind the children. For easy figuring, let us assume both man and woman worked forty hours—the difference being the tasks and that the woman's labor was unpaid. When women entered the workforce, adding additional hours (now paid) to their total work, the system did not respond with childcare centers, easy-prep meals, and an expectation that household chores would now be evenly shared. The assumption was simply that women would keep doing what they were doing in addition to the privilege of working for pay. They would have to figure out how it all came together. And that is pretty much how it remains today.

We can sidestep the often-sensitive subject of who does what in partnered households and simply agree that women consistently do significantly more unpaid work than men. Sadly, the percentage has remained about the same over the decades. Women in developed nations spend an average of 4.3 hours *each day* doing unpaid labor.[26] That can be all kinds of things, like cooking, shopping, childcare, transportation, helping with homework, laundry, home maintenance, decorating, yard work, banking, scheduling appointments, tending to older parents, and entertaining. As we all know, it is endless—more than four hours a day just to keep the wheels rolling.

In contrast, men in developed nations spend an average of 1.5 hours doing unpaid labor in the home.[27]

It is interesting to note the difference between developed nations and developing nations. The total amount of unpaid labor is much less in developed nations; however, only for men, not for women.[28]

---

26 Department of Economic and Social Affairs, *The World's Women 2015: Trends and Statistics* (New York: United Nations, 2015), 112, unstats.un.org/unsd/gender/downloads/worldswomen2015_report.pdf.

27 *The World's Women 2015*, 112.

28 *The World's Women 2015*, 112.

This reminds us of how unyielding the gender divide remains when it comes to who does what in the home.

As you look at the graphic below, imagine with me, if you will, what women's lives might include but for those 4.3 additional work hours each day. Make a mental list of all the things one might do, all the moments of repose, play, learning, dreaming, or even focused work on a passion or hobby that could be had. All those things are nourishment in comparison to the soul-sucking depletion of mundane, repetitive, unnoticed, and unappreciated unpaid labor.

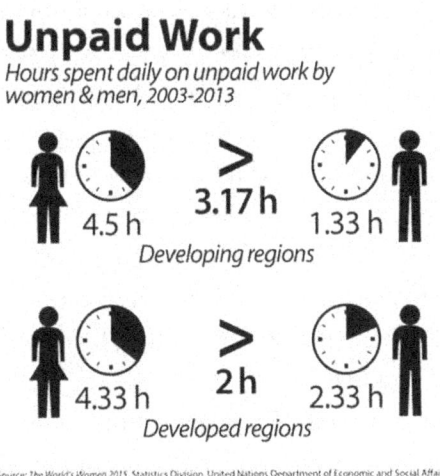

Figure 1: "Unpaid Work" graphic courtesy of Rosamond Hutt, World Economic Forum, 2015.

WITNESSING THE ENCUMBRANCES

It was as the gender equity coordinator at a local technical college that I first started seeing, up close, how women are unfairly encumbered on every front and thinking about the changes needed in public policy as remedy. The challenges for a single person just out of high school were so much different from those of a single mother trying to ramp up her skills to get a good-paying job. Gwen, one of the students at the college, could not have made this point any clearer.

Gwen was a single mother of three living in Limington, Maine, about a forty-five-minute drive from campus. Before driving to school every day, she had to get her children up, feed them breakfast, pack their lunches, and get them off to three different schools. She got her high schooler and middle schooler on their buses and then drove her third child to primary school before she headed to class herself.

Occasionally, she would be a couple of minutes late to class. *No wonder!* Yet one of her professors had a policy that if you were even one minute late, you could come in to sit and listen, but none of the work that you did that day would be graded. In other words, she would get a zero.

My job, as the gender equity coordinator, was to reach out to female students and offer them additional support. At the time, the support I had to offer was just a listening ear. I gathered together a handful of women that I recruited from the hallways and asked them to come in to talk a bit about the challenges they had as older students. It became quickly obvious that the biggest challenge wasn't age so much as the responsibilities of parenthood, in particular single parenthood, which fell overwhelmingly to women. In fact, the entire time I was there, I met only one single dad who was caring for children.

Gwen told me about not always being able to be on time and how that was a detriment to her, and we made a plan to bring it up to the faculty to try to draw the distinction between a nineteen-year-old man rolling out of his dorm five minutes before class and the hours that Gwen had to spend before she could even get in her car and head to school. Our discussion with the faculty was met with believable concern but no commitment to action.

That moment right then was when I started seeing clearly through the gender lens. I saw so many of the institutional bumps and barriers that women were up against at the college and beyond, and I clearly understood that a listening, even concerned, ear was far from enough. I joined with other like minds to attack the system that so encumbered a woman's success.

We called ourselves the Coalition of Women in Trades and Technology, a group of like-minded women from various places in government, academia, the welfare system, and the Maine Equal Justice organization, as well as representatives of the industries most likely to employ the women when they finished their training and education. Our goal was to press the many and various institutions and traditions to rethink, retool, and re-rig the system to address inequities and barriers—starting with the new federal welfare-to-work law.

WELFARE-TO-WORK

The new federal law—the Personal Responsibility and Work Opportunity Reconciliation Act of 1996—discouraged states from incorporating post-secondary education into their individual state welfare programs and focused instead on work-first policies. "These restrictions had a devastating impact on the three-quarters of a million welfare recipients in college: decreases in enrollment among recipients ranged from 29 percent to 82 percent".[29] Hundreds of thousands of low-income mothers across the country were forced to drop out of college and find jobs in order to comply with strict work-first welfare rules.

It is difficult to understand if this law was enacted out of ignorance of the reality of poor women or disdain. Did Congress not believe that an education would improve a family's financial circumstances? Or were they simply counting on women's invisibility in the public space as they slashed through the budget, cutting down on opportunities for women to pull themselves out of poverty?

Our group started to work to advocate for change. We focused on what we affectionately referred to as the "ticking clock." Women and their children could go on welfare and receive benefits, but after two years,

---

29 Johanna Finney, "Welfare Reform and Post-secondary Education: Research and Policy Update," *IWPR Welfare Reform Network News* 2, no. 1 (1998): 2, quoted in Sandra S. Butler and Luisa S. Deprez, "The Parents as Scholars Program: A Maine Success Story," *Maine Policy Review* 17, no. 1 (2008): 41, digitalcommons.library. umaine.edu/mpr/vol17/iss1/7.

the new law stated, they would be dropped from the welfare rolls. Obviously, there was no magic that happened in two years unless women were engaged in a plan to be self-sustaining after that, and—surprisingly or not—there was no education or effort to support such a plan. Policymakers imagined that the threat of being abandoned after two years of support would be enough to move the women from poverty to prosperity.

Since the late 1990s, to receive benefits, one must be looking for work or prove that there isn't work available.[30] Additionally, children were covered under Medicaid/welfare while their mothers received benefits, but if the mothers were to take even a minimum-wage job, they could exceed the limit of what they could earn and would thus lose their children's healthcare. This created an astounding bind and is another example of how women had to be extraordinary to manage under these circumstances.

Think of that giant leap of faith. We were asking them to jump into low-wage work with an uncertain future in order to beat the alarm of the ticking clock—they would lose their food stamps, their children's health coverage, *and* the childcare stipend they received—and hope that the low-wage job might develop into something sustainable, providing enough money to afford childcare, food, and eventually provide healthcare benefits. It was a near-impossible ask. The technical college was the perfect place to stage this policy-changing effort, as its mission was to equip people for well-paying jobs in two years.

As it happened, there was a big gender divide in the programs and their relative pay structures. The plumbing, heating, drafting, and firefighting courses were overwhelmingly populated by men, and the average pay of those jobs was significantly higher than the nursing aides, office technology, and childcare worker programs. Here we were again at the boy jobs/girl jobs dichotomy.

Welfare's two-year ticking clock made it apparent we had to find ways to move women quickly to well-paying jobs. One of our goals was

---

30 Anne Kim, "Welfare Work Requirements Have to Go," Washington Monthly, April 17, 2021, washingtonmonthly.com/2021/04/17/welfare-work-requirements-have-to-go/.

to convince women to get into these male-dominated areas. The resistance from the school, as well as from the other students—and a bit from the women themselves—was immense.

One of the incentives that Maine's women's advocates were able to build was a Medicaid waiver that allowed us to turn off that ticking clock as long as the recipient was enrolled in a course of education that had a high probability of a job with a living wage on the other end of it. If you were taking art history, your clock would keep ticking, but if you were taking computer drafting, you could continue to receive benefits past that two-year mark.

Our coalition of committed upstart women began to meet, plan, write, plot, and ultimately execute our strategy. We wanted to show the plight of women trying to better themselves economically and just how difficult that was. Additionally, we wanted to present an option and show the benefits of it to the economy in general, as well as to the women and their families.

Gwen's Story

My primary job in this effort was to gather women who were struggling and enlist them to provide information and ultimately testify to the value of the Medicaid waiver so that they could locate themselves to a better place in the economy.

I found sixteen women at the technical college, all of them single parents, all of them struggling, and all of them worried about what was at the end of their two years. On the day that we were to travel to the state capital to present testimony on the legislation that was to support the Medicaid waiver, I invited the women to my office for coffee and doughnuts before we took off. In the weeks before, I had helped them with their testimony, inviting them to use my office to type it up and print it. I was also there to give them advice if they wanted it.

Of the sixteen women, only twelve showed up at the office that morning. By the end of the coffee break, eight had decided they would go forward and actually make the hour drive to Augusta to testify. A few of them were carpooling, but most were driving themselves. We agreed to meet in front of the legislative committee room.

When I arrived, no one was there. I got very nervous. Finally, after a long half hour, Gwen showed up. She was one of only three women who actually made the trip and ended up being the only one who testified.

She was understandably nervous as she listened to the various legislators, faculty members, and advocacy groups present their testimony. We all knew that hers would be the most compelling, as she would be a direct recipient of the benefits of this legislation. The pressure was showing on her face. She asked if I would read her testimony for her. I said I would but that they really wanted to hear from her and that that would be most compelling of all. I asked her to trust me.

As she stood up to the microphone, her hands were visibly shaking. Her voice was trembling. She kept having to take deep breaths, and she couldn't hold her papers still enough to read. I got up next to her and took the testimony from her hands, and I whispered in her ear, "Just tell them what your day is like, tell them what your week is like, and tell them why you are going to college."

Imagine yourself there in that environment. It is almost designed to be intimidating. The committee sits in a half-circle. You are in the middle, at a podium with a microphone. The people you are speaking to all have "Honorable" in front of their names. Two of the people in the semicircle have gavels, and they occasionally hit them to ask a person to desist or to put the committee in recess. It is a very intimidating construct for anyone. It is not welcoming.

Gwen took a deep breath and looked straight up at the committee members and said:

> "I wish I were dressed a little better for this today. I'm wearing this very large shirt not because I'm overweight, but because I'm not wearing a bra. I'm not wearing a bra because the one I have been

wearing and holding together with safety pins and a stitch here and there finally gave out this morning—there was nothing left to pin. I don't know how many of you have recently purchased a bra, but they are very expensive and just not something I can afford right now.

"I live in Limington, Maine. It is forty-five minutes from school. And before I get to school, I have to wake my children, feed them breakfast, make their lunches and my own, and get them all to three different schools—one in high school, one in middle school, and one in elementary.

"I'm studying computer drafting and I love it, and I'm looking forward to graduating and having a good-paying job where I can support my kids, make sure they have healthcare, and show them that hard work really pays off.

"I hate being on welfare. I wouldn't be on welfare if my kids didn't need what they need. I'm not lazy. It isn't that I don't wanna work; it's that I know a $7-an-hour job is gonna keep us poor for the rest of our lives, and my kids deserve more than that.

"So, what I want you to know is I am committed to my education. I am committed to supporting myself and my children, but it isn't easy. Every month—every single month—I get a little bit behind. Actually, last month was the best month I've had in a year—everything went well. I didn't have any car trouble, I didn't have to stay home from class with a sick child, and there was nothing in the house that needed fixing, and at the end of the month I had $7.00 left over. I got to use six of those dollars to sign my son up for Cub Scouts.

"If I get kicked off of welfare before I finish my course and find a job, I don't know what will happen to me and my children. I know that if I have to work a $7.00 [an hour] job I will.[31] I know

---

31 "History of Federal Minimum Wage Rates Under the Fair Labor Standards Act, 1938 – 2009," U.S. Department of Labor, accessed December 13, 2021, www.dol.gov/agencies/whd/minimum-wage/history/chart.

that if I can't go back on welfare and they need to eat, I will find a way to feed them, and if they get sick, I will figure out a way to take care of them. What I would want you to know is that people like me are not sitting home being grateful that we don't have to work, watching soap operas and eating bonbons. We're doing everything we can to better ourselves in spite of these systems and programs that most people think we don't deserve. It's really hard—" Her voice broke. "It's really hard."

The committee room was quiet. There was a moment before one of the committee members spoke and thanked Gwen for her testimony and for her courage. Another member on the committee told her she had given him a glimpse into something that he had not really imagined until then. But sadly, the chair of the committee, just before she left the room and handed the gavel to someone else, said, "Well, I'm from Aroostook County, and we don't like welfare up there. If I don't have a cup of sugar, I borrow it from my neighbor. And if my neighbor needs a cup of sugar, she can borrow it from me. And if kids need taking care of, you can take care of her kids in the morning while she works, and she can take care of your kids at night while you work."

The woman was well-heeled, well-dressed, and well-versed in disdain of welfare, and quite comfortable demeaning Gwen and others like her. Needless to say, no one else got up to offer their testimony.

That was the moment I decided that I was tired of trying to lobby the wrong people to do the right thing and that no amount of testimony or data or heartbreak or hope on this side of the microphone was going to convince those who chose not to be convinced that what is good for women is good for families, and what is good for families is good for the economy. That was when I decided to actively campaign for people who cared about the things I cared about, and to get the right people elected.

Looking back, I realize that it was Gwen and women like her who inspired my advocacy work from that point on. Like my grandmothers, her strength and love for family drove her to be extraordinary simply to survive. She humanized what was impossible to describe on spreadsheets and with facts and figures. She made sure that we could see her, and I will submit that anyone with an honest and open mind could never unsee her.

COMPETENCE VERSUS QUALIFICATION: WOMEN'S SELF-CONFIDENCE AS ENCUMBRANCE

One of the women in our lobbying group, whose groundbreaking report underpinned our advocacy work by describing the labor market opportunities available and not available to low-skilled working women, was an economist at the University of Maine.[32] She reminded us that one of the obstacles we had to overcome was the attitudes of the women themselves. Even though we could equip women with the skills so that they were qualified to do what were then called "men's jobs," we were not as successful at equipping them with confidence. Surely this, too, was a result of generational, systemic conditioning.

She taught us about a study that asked a simple question of a large sample of men and women with regard to their competence. The inquiry was "What percentage of your job do you need to know before you would call yourself competent?" This study has been replicated, and the percentages remain remarkably the same over time. Before I reveal the answer, ask yourself the question and fix the number in your mind.

Women, unsurprisingly, say they need to know 100% of the job before they would call themselves competent. Men, on the other hand, say 60%, adding that they'll learn the rest as they go along. It seems men can accept themselves as qualified and will learn competence on the job, whereas women want to arrive with it—and employers hold that expectation, too.[33]

---

32 Stephanie Seguino, "Living on the Edge: Women Working and Providing for Families in the Maine Economy, 1979–1993," Maine Policy Review 17, no. 1 (1995): 43.

33 Tara Sophia Mohr, "Why Women Don't Apply for Jobs Unless They're 100% Qualified," Harvard Business Review, August 25, 2014, hbr.org/2014/08/why-women-dont-apply-for-jobs-unless-theyre-100-qualified.

Here is a real-world example of that phenomenon: One of the women in our group working on welfare reform told us about a conversation with her son after he came home from high school with a posting he had gotten from the guidance counselor on summer job possibilities. He showed it to her with excitement about how much money he could make. She looked at it and said, "But, honey, this says you have to have sheet metal experience, and you don't have sheet metal experience."

He replied, "Mom, don't you remember that dustpan I made you in shop class?"

As funny as that is, it is exactly what we are up against. Women in general would never call making a shop class dustpan sheet metal experience. And, if we did, the market would likely demand proof. There is no shortage of studies that show that men are hired for their potential—or what the employer can imagine them doing—and the skill sets and experience that they have. Women, in great part, are hired for the *proof* of what they can do or what they have already done.[34]

This is partly because of what is called "the halo effect."[35] If the employer/interviewer sees someone in front of them who resembles them, they imagine their success. If they see someone different—whether based on gender, race, socioeconomic status, age, etc.—it is more difficult for them to imagine the person succeeding. They resort to thinking: "OK, show me what you can do or what you have done. What makes you think you can do this job?" How many of us have been asked that question?

There are two things at work here that conspire to reinforce each other: women's lack of confidence in their competence and employers' habit of responding to men's confidence as evidence of competence.

---

34 Katty Kay and Claire Shipman, "The Confidence Gap," The Atlantic, April 15, 2014, www.theatlantic.com/magazine/archive/2014/05/the-confidence-gap/359815/.

35 Robert Half, "What Is the Halo-Effect and How Can It Impact Interviews?," Robert Half, November 9, 2021, www.roberthalf.com.au/blog/employers/hiring-and-halo-effect-trap.

Men are much more likely to overestimate their competence, while women underestimate theirs. And though we know this intuitively, we can also point to scholarship that confirms it.

> "A review of personnel records found that women working at HP applied for a promotion only when they believed they met 100 percent of the qualifications listed for the job. Men were happy to apply when they thought they could meet 60 percent of the job requirements. At HP, and in study after study, the data confirm what we instinctively know. Underqualified and underprepared men don't think twice about applying. Overqualified and overprepared, too many women still hold back."[36]

HIGH EXPECTATIONS, LOW SUPPORT

While in the Maine Legislature and for a brief time after, I served on the board of a very successful program for at-risk teenagers. These kids were from single-parent homes, in poverty, in trouble with the law, or had behavioral problems at school. Over time, we conducted a study to track the success of our students five years after graduation compared with the general high school population. Based on pay and the percentage who went on to get a post-secondary education, we found that our kids outperformed the kids who were not labeled at risk.

Our next question was, "What was it about our program that delivered these results?" Many of us, at one time, had volunteered at programs where things had been dumbed down and students were babied, hoping to remediate them to the level of the more fortunate students of their age or class, but our program was different. Every day, we offered them high touch, high support, and—this was critically important—high expectations. The equation worked every time.

But what if we had expected these students to perform less well than the more fortunate ones? What if we had required that they show us their

---

36 Kay and Shipman, "The Confidence Gap."

competence instead of simply expecting it? We know this answer. We live this, and the studies and articles we can point to confirm it.

It doesn't require a big imagination to picture oneself a woman in a job where the workforce doesn't particularly welcome you, or at least they are not used to you, you have an additional four hours a day of unpaid labor on your plate, and your confidence is 40% less than that of the men you work with—and *still* there are women who succeed by every measure, even with odds stacked so heavily against their success.

Now imagine our levels of success and joy, our feelings of abundance and accomplishment, if we:

- could count on support and nourishment
- were expected to deliver a high-quality result
- didn't have to constantly strategize, prioritize, and reprioritize our needs and our family's needs
- could count on reliable, affordable, high-quality childcare
- didn't have to make a grocery list or plan a week of meals and lunches while assuring that birthdays were noted, cards sent, car inspected, presents wrapped, the plow guy paid, the doctor's appointment made, etc.

What might we do with the energy we currently use to try to make a hostile environment less so? What might we do with all that extra time? What might we do with the extra $0.23 on every dollar earned in an atmosphere of gender equity? If all these things were easily accessible to women, I submit that the books and courses and articles on women's empowerment would not be the industry it is.

We would understand *it is not us*. It is not our fault that we are exhausted and scrambling to keep up. It is *no wonder*. We are not weak and in need of an infusion of power; we are simply overburdened and undernourished. High expectations of ourselves and each other, with no support, is not an equation for sustainable success, yet we keep trying it.

Our Response to the Stacked Deck

When my grandmother Nanny B. was first looking for a job, she had to prove that she had not only the qualifications but also the logistical support at home to manage her house and children. There was no way for her to point out this unfairness and *also* get the job. No one wanted to hire her, and her plight was no one's responsibility but hers. Whatever her husband (eventual ex-husband) did not provide was completely her responsibility, whether she could find work or not.

The plight of women today is arguably better, but not by much. We have been acculturated into the world of work with the notion that we are fortunate if we have a well-paying job. We demonstrate that we deserve the job with our extraordinary performance, ideas, insights, cost-saving measures, and our willingness to go above and beyond. We do this long after we have secured the job; it becomes our daily way of working rather than a sprint of excellence to prove our qualifications. Before we know it, we women have become chronic overworkers.

It can be confounding to think about the real and perceived gains that have been made for women in the past few decades and try to square that with our frustration and fatigue and considerable discomfort. In her article, "Why Women Still Can't Have It All," Anne-Marie Slaughter points to the work of two economists who studied what they referred to as "the paradox of *women's* declining relative well-being," noting that "although women as a group have made substantial gains in wages, educational attainment, and prestige over the past three decades, these economists, Justin Wolfers and Betsey Stevenson, have shown that women are less happy today than their predecessors were in 1972, both in absolute terms and relative to men."[37]

To repeat myself: Women do not need to be empowered so much as they need to be unencumbered. Unfettered from this invisible, generational suppression, and with the time and money our male colleagues may

---

[37] Anne-Marie Slaughter, "Why Women Still Can't Have It All," The Atlantic, June 13, 2012, www.theatlantic.com/magazine/archive/2012/07/why-women-still-cant-have-it-all/309020/.

well take for granted, our self-development and our impact on the world would be limitless.

Or would it?

Next, let's take a look at how we buy into the system and the alternatives to doing so.

Lynn's Hamster Wheel

In the early 2000s, after working as an advocate for economic equity for women, I became disenchanted with our ability to make the proper points to the proper people in the Maine Legislature and the federal government.

My short-term answer was that, instead of trying to get the wrong people to do the right thing, I would work on people's campaigns. In other words, I would elect the right people to do the right thing. It was not a very long walk from there to my longer-term solution: realizing that I was one of those right people and that my knowledge and experience would be beneficial in our state's legislature.

I decided to run for office in the state senate. It was not that Maine did not have women in the legislature; it did. But there were no women with full-time jobs, or many with jobs at all. Nor were there many of us with school-age children. In fact, there were only three of us: two women and one man (whose wife was at home full time).

Maine prides itself on its citizen legislature. By tradition, the state's legislature was made up of farmers, fishermen, and foresters. They worked near their homes in the summer months and the warm weather and then headed to the state capital in January for six months to do the work of the people before they returned to the fields, forests, and the sea. Maine still maintains the same legislative schedule based on the agrarian calendar, and citizen legislators are paid a stipend and expenses. So, it is impossible to have legislating be your full-time job; though, it is a full-time job. Many of the members are lawyers or doctors or retired. They are either wealthy or their livelihood is derivative to a partner or other family member. They are mostly men.

When I first started thinking about running, I was recruited by a group of progressives who believed that there ought to be more women in the legislature. I was asked to join a class to learn how to run for office. The first handful of meetings established the premise that it was important for women to be at the table as policy was being made, particularly as much of that policy had to do with children, families, and healthcare. Those were issues of great importance to families, and thus women needed to be a part of the discussion.

I had no argument with that and felt very affirmed by the message. But the tone in the room and the curriculum soon changed to explaining how we needed to be empowered as women in order to run. That we needed to be *convinced* we were good enough and that we had something to say or something to offer. At the time, this was slightly uncomfortable. In retrospect, I understand this as a dangerous myth: that women need to *be empowered.* That we need to be reminded that what is second nature to us might not be to men, that we have value, that our voices should be heard, that we should speak up. All the while the system recruiting us, and that we were going to be delivered to, was not expecting us, was not rigged in our favor, and was not welcoming to us—beginning with the campaign and certainly continuing while we served in office.

Because I was not wealthy and my income was necessary for my family, I had to work part time, take care of my children part time, and campaign part time. It was three part-time jobs, each of them requiring well over twenty hours a week. I hoped that I could extend the childcare I had arranged during my workday with campaign contributions.

Sadly, I learned that childcare was not an authorized expense for campaigns, making the proverbial playing field even more uneven. When men with children ran for office, they most often had wives or partners at home taking care of them. I tried to assert that if campaign funds could not be used to pay for childcare, then at least uncompensated childcare should be treated like other in-kind donations to a campaign (e.g., free office space, loaned furniture, consulting), and the fair market value of that childcare ought to be tallied and included on our campaign expense reports.

That notion was considered outrageous. Paying for childcare with campaign funds was just as illegal as using that money for a weekend holiday in the Bahamas. One of my own campaign volunteers told me that if I could not afford to get my kids taken care of, then I probably should not run for office.

As I think back to campaign school, I wonder why those advocacy efforts to convince women to run for office were not focused on the structural issues of why it is more difficult for women to run for office. Instead of just telling women how much we are needed, tell us that we are going to have to find our own childcare, that the hours will be long, that people will dismiss us and our ideas, that we will be appointed to low-level committees unless we do something outstanding to show our worth and worthiness to our caucus—and help us build a plan and strategy to overcome all that.

My only way to run for office (and ultimately win) was to be extraordinary, and to be extraordinary every single day. To be willing and able to work extra time to make my contribution to the family pot, to take care of my children when I was not working and my husband was, and then to campaign around the edges, on weekends and evenings when my husband was home instead of during the day when most candidates were out there.

There is a tradition in New England when you are campaigning for local office. You knock on people's doors, give them printed information, and have a conversation with them so they get to know you a bit, and you get to understand what is important to your soon-to-be constituents. During my first campaign, I learned that, if elected, I would be the first Democrat in the history of my state to serve my district. I was an unknown. I had never been on the school board or served in any public capacity, so my plan was to knock on as many doors as possible and have as many high-quality conversations as I could. I knocked on 5,280 doors, burned up a couple of pairs of sneakers, and managed lots of volunteers as I worked the equivalent of three jobs, working overtime to exhaustion on many days. It was the price I was willing to pay, and *had* to pay, to be a woman without means running for office.

And I won. I loved my work in the senate. It was difficult financially and logistically, and my time away from my children weighed heavily on me. My daily commute to the state capital and back was 126 miles. Many of my colleagues stayed in Augusta during the week and returned home on the weekends. Those of us with school-age children, however, commuted daily with the exception of budget time, when we worked into the night and I was sometimes too exhausted to drive home. I loved the work, but exhaustion was a constant companion.

The primary cost of chronic overwork sustained at a high level over time is fatigue and exhaustion. It is the overwhelmingly constant denominator reported by women. Simply being a woman is a preexisting condition for exhaustion.

If this were a screenplay for a dystopian movie, I might make this point by writing about how the world ended when women finally wore themselves out. They were no longer able to work beyond the norm and, sadly, men had evolved into soft beings no longer equipped with sufficient physical and mental strength to do the work. Thus, things started to fall apart, leading to the demise of the human race.

Or I could write a movie with a more utopian plot about the establishment, or reestablishment, of matriarchy as a preferred societal structure in recognition of the superiority of women as thinkers and doers.

Or perhaps a simple reiteration of the real-life example of how, in 1975, the women of Iceland virtually stopped their economy when they went on strike for a day to protest the lack of value given to their unpaid labor and their invisibility in elected office and public policy. They refused to work, cook, or look after children for a day. It was called "Women's Day Off" by the women and "The Long Friday" by the men. It was a moment that changed the way women were seen in the country and helped put Iceland at the forefront of the fight for equality.

To be clear, the primary purpose of this book is not to suggest matriarchy as an alternative to our current system, or to suggest what we all should be doing in order to deliver ourselves and each other from injustice, as justice will not arrive overnight. It is, instead, to suggest and demonstrate the importance of a sisterhood so that we are nourishing ourselves and each other on the path to justice.

Though we support much-needed concrete changes in policy and practice, our short-term success metrics will not be the usual stubbornly static numbers like the percentage of women in elected office, an increase in women's total wages, the number of women on boards of directors, the percentage of venture capital that goes to women-owned businesses, or even the increase in affordable and accessible childcare, healthcare, and education. We will focus, instead, on the metrics assessed in the informal survey that has partially informed this book.[38]

The survey asked these questions:

- How often do you experience exhaustion?

- How often do you experience frustration?

- Are you in a state of being chronically extraordinary?

- How often do you feel joy?

- How often do you feel contentment?

- How often do you feel fulfillment? At work? At home?

- Do you feel supported by women?

As an example, responses to the survey indicated that 50% of respondents noted depression "frequently," 60% noted feeling exhausted "frequently," and 30% said they were exhausted "always." These are the metrics we want to affect now. Here is where a sisterhood can move the needle immediately. Simply being a woman ought not be a preexisting

---

[38] Designed and conducted by myself.

condition for depression and exhaustion. That is not sustainable in our lives or in our culture.

But does this really work—a sisterhood?

In a word, YES!

In small individual ways, nearly immediately. Small in action, but nonetheless transformative.

In group action, more gradually, and in large systematic ways—some with immediacy but most to be determined. To be determined in great part by you and the sisterhood that you inspire and the path that you point to and widen.

CHAPTER 4

How We Work Against Ourselves

Before we can become part of the solution, we have to acknowledge how we participate in the problem. We need to be clear about how women have accepted the cultural conditioning of extraordinariness and bought into the very system that holds us down.

We can begin by thinking about the extra qualifications and experience that women expect of themselves and each other. We want to perform 100% of the job before we will declare ourselves competent compared with men's 60%. This shows up as women willing to work longer in a job before they expect or seek a salary increase or promotion.

In addition to this lag in our full participation, women are also likely to exclude themselves from applying for jobs that they are equipped to perform. Fiona Lee, a PhD candidate at Stanford's Clayman Institute for Gender Research, posed the following question in her research: "Imagine you have a once-in-a-lifetime opportunity to apply for your dream job, but there's a catch: You have most—but not all—of the qualifications the employers want. Do you take a chance and apply?"[39]

Her research confirmed yet another example of women working against themselves. She found that "women show a reluctance to apply for jobs when they do not meet all the requirements listed in the job

---

39 Julia Sakowitz, "Uncovering the Gendered Dimensions of Job Hunting," The Clayman Institute for Gender Research, February 28, 2018, gender.stanford.edu/news-publications/gender-news/uncovering-gendered-dimensions-job-hunting.

advertisement. Women express a far greater need to fulfill **all** the noted job requirements in an advertisement before applying than men do. Lee posits that this gender difference might reflect 'women's belief that they need to be perfect in the eyes of potential employers in order to compete with men.' More importantly, it simply leaves women out of the equation when they pass up chances to apply for jobs for fear of not being qualified enough."[40]

If you are reading this and you are an employer, particularly if you have ever thought or said, "I wanted to hire a woman, but none applied," consider carefully the wording in your job postings. Is the list of desired skills and experience brief or read like a list of the types of attributes you are looking for in a candidate? Or is there wording that describes wanting a person who can bring skills and perspectives to share and who has interest and excitement about learning more?

WE EXPECT NO PAY OR LOW PAY FOR MANY OF THE THINGS WE DO

When asked to moderate or serve on a panel, speak at a conference, or write a proposal, women are often willing to fulfill the request pro bono without question. We assume that we will do it for nothing as the default and are surprised when we get paid for these sorts of things. How many times have I been asked to speak and said yes before I even inquired about the terms? More than I'd like to admit.

In 2016, I attended a conference for women in business with a group of women colleagues. As we compared our experiences at the conference, we began to express our disappointment to each other about the workshop offerings. In particular, though most of the moderating was done by women, we were bothered by the dominance of men both presenting individually as well as populating the dreaded "manels" (all-male panels).[41]

---

40 Mohr, "Why Women Don't Apply for Jobs Unless They're 100% Qualified."

41 "Only Men at Your Event? This Blog Will Shame You," BBC, May 27, 2015, www.bbc.com/news/blogs-trending-32789580.

Men cast as experts and women as facilitators. We brought this to the attention of the organizers, and they were quick to offer us the opportunity to curate content for an upcoming conference.

We were excited to start imagining the experience we might create as we began to list ideas for relevant topics and people—women—we knew whom we would like to invite to speak and present. Our excitement quickly waned as we were offered the last two spots on the last day of a three-day conference and no budget.

I thought it was important to make the point that content designed with women in mind was important—so much so that I was willing to do it for no pay. We recruited some like-minded people and decided to reach out to a dynamic speaker in order to promote our late-in-the-day workshop. We agreed to contact Cindy Gallop, founder and former chair of the US branch of the advertising firm Bartle Bogle Hegarty and founder of IfWeRanTheWorld and MakeLoveNotPorn, as we knew she would draw a crowd.

I am embarrassed to remember my request that she accept a travel stipend (a very small one) as we did not have a budget. She very gently declined, saying simply: "I charge for my speaking time, and though I applaud your cause, I am not taking on any pro bono work at this time."

That was the last time I ever asked a woman to do what she does for a living for nothing. I might ask for a discount or what I might refer to as the "family price," or even note that our speaker budget can accommodate only a modest stipend, but "nothing" would never again be my offer. How can I advocate for gender equity if I assume that women's time and talent ought to be unpaid?

It is notable that when men perform what is traditionally "women's work," we are much less likely to assume that they might be unpaid. A Swedish economist, Katrine Marçal, writes in her book *Who Cooked Adam Smith's Dinner?* about a visiting American economist in Stockholm who, after walking around the city and seeing many men pushing baby carriages, asks her Swedish host, "What's up with all the gay nannies?"

These men were, of course, not nannies at all but rather the fathers of the children they were minding, most of them on paternity leave.[42] We would not assume a woman pushing a carriage was a nanny, i.e., getting paid for her time, but we do when it is a man.

The Lie of the Empowerment Industry

Take a stroll through a bookstore and head to the self-help section. Notice the number of books with the words *empowerment* and *women* in the titles. List the titles, or better yet, make a collage of the covers. These books promise us success and happiness—or at least hint at it—if we think and act differently. If we do everything extraordinarily.

In our workplaces, we are encouraged to lean in, speak clearly, stand up straight, wash our faces, and learn how to negotiate for a raise. If we want a mentor, we are told to make ourselves indispensable to our bosses instead. Other books offer checklists and strategies to do more in less time in our homes. How to be more organized and how to plan our meals for the week—of course, making sure that our ingredients are nutritious, organic, and locally sourced. There are parenting books with strategies that range from how to listen to your children all the way to tough love, and how to make your home more inviting so it becomes the one on the street the kids want to hang out in—nutritious after-school snacks included, naturally.

The books I keep buying are the ones that promise a clean house in just fifteen minutes a day. The most recent one details how one must first spend a couple of hours on a "one-time total clean" on each room and enlist other family members in scheduled chores before the fifteen minutes each day will work effectively. I have three of these books in a dusty pile in my kitchen, as well as an online membership to Mrs. Somebody's daily tips on keeping a clean and orderly house. At least I *think* I still have the online membership. I do not know for sure, as I have not checked for so long.

When I am overwhelmed with thinking and doing, I wish for an

---

42 Katrine Marçal, *Who Cooked Adam Smith's Dinner?: A Story of Women and Economics*, trans. Saskia Vogel (New York: Pegasus Books, 2016), vi.

organized mind and a to-do list, but I cannot seem to make myself take the time to write it. Despite a long history of this tactic not working, I imagine that a pristine home and office will solve the problem. Perhaps it would help if it were to magically appear. My start-and-stop attempts at new methods suggested in the many books and articles in my "should do" library do little except to add more tasks to my already too long list and deliver me an additional sense of failure.

The books that feel the most insulting to the lives of so many women are the ones that tell us to be sure to take time for ourselves but do not acknowledge that if we do take time for ourselves, we will have to let something else go. Have a bath with scented candles, "let Calgon take you away," as the TV ad used to say. But do I take that bath at the cost of bathing my child or spending time with my partner?

The empowerment books I believe are the most dangerous are the ones that promise we can think ourselves into success and happiness. Illness, poverty, lack of training and education, discrimination, and oppression will not be solved by our thinking our way into happiness. Let us instead begin by thinking that we—all of us—deserve success and happiness and that our constant, chronic struggle to do more and be better is a *really bad deal* for women.

As we overfunction—as we require ourselves and each other to be extraordinary—we help to maintain a system that survives on the underpaid (or unpaid) and undervalued work of women. The economic system supported by patriarchy and gender disparity works pretty well for the few and powerful. As long as we continue to believe that self-improvement and hard work will solve institutional inequities and yield success for us, the status quo will remain.

How We Participate in a Really Bad Deal

The solution presented in this book is less about smashing patriarchy and more about challenging the social code and norms that patriarchy has spawned because we are participants in that system.

Here is a list of some of the ways we work against our own best interests:

- We embrace and allow for the continuous push to be extraordinary—and **we judge ourselves and others** for not succeeding. We often make these judgments silently, but we sometimes give them voice.

- We **deny our global competence**. When we are able to do a job or task or have a relationship that is a bit above average, we discount it—sometimes totally. We do not even consider ourselves as a candidate for something more than what we are doing. The world is run on mediocre energy performed by mediocre talent. We know this, yet we still somehow demand more of ourselves.

- We **undervalue our work** and allow others to do the same.

- We **work beyond our job descriptions,** pouring passion and skill into tasks where we are not seen and for which we are not rewarded.

- We are **careless with our language**. This is an insidious habit that likely stems from the old convention and expectation that women be modest. Consider how we sometimes take a compliment as simple as "I really like that sweater; it's a great color on you." How often have you said or heard something like "Oh, this old thing? I picked it up at Goodwill years ago and just found it in the back of my closet." When we think or speak about ourselves negatively, we give permission to others to do the same.

- **We say yes too much**. This is what Anne-Marie Slaughter refers to as the "culture of the presumptive yes."[43] How many times have you accepted a task when you were already working near or at capacity to a titter in the room of "If you want something done, give it to a busy person and it will get done." That busy person is most often a woman who is uncomfortable or unaccustomed to declining or suggesting that a less-busy person might be a better fit.

---

43 Slaughter, "Why Women Still Can't Have It All."

- A close cousin to that is **the reluctance to say no**. I recall two very powerful lessons that I still carry very close to me. I learned them from two very different women. The first was my daughter when she was about twenty. I overheard her on the phone. It was clear that someone was asking her to do something or go somewhere. She said, "Ah, no, that's not going to work for me." I listened closer, waiting to hear her reason, and *she didn't give one*. It was stunning and exciting to imagine doing that myself, thinking of the years I had spent feeling the need to give a reason or excuse, to explain myself, to justify not doing or doing, and imagining that there was no other way.

  The second lesson came from Sonia, a no-nonsense woman who had been advocating for workers' rights for much of her career as a union rep. We were part of a volunteer group working on a gay rights campaign. Someone asked her if she could manage the training and staffing of the phone banks.

  She asked, "Who else can provide some leadership for this?" No one answered, as we all thought she was clearly the best choice.

  She added, "Well, I can provide the leadership if others manage the implementation." Still no volunteers, so she said, "It seems we don't have sufficient support to take this on." There were protests about how important it was and how we all had to do all we could, as the mission was so important.

  She didn't take the bait but instead said, "Well, I will continue to attend these meetings and provide some guidance and suggestions, but I won't be able to do any take-away tasks."

  It was impressive, and I was again stunned to see a woman decline a task that was not sufficiently supported instead of taking it on with the strategy of overworking and hoping to figure it out along the way. I keep Sonia close to whisper in my ear whenever I find myself in this situation.

- **We accept isolation and individualism as the norm**. This happens in two main ways. One is that being chronically extraordinary is not inclusive; it involves toxic competition. We separate ourselves from others so that the "best" of us get noticed, rise to the surface, and secure our position. Then we can become models of how to "succeed." The other is by distancing ourselves from our sisters.

Here is where I need to make a long-overdue apology. In my first management job, I was counseled by my boss to no longer sit with my girlfriends at lunch. He said I would not be taken seriously if I hung out with the "hourly" people rather than the directors and managers, who were, of course, all men. He noted that I was "not like the other girls" and that was, in part, why I was promoted—I did not make the men feel uncomfortable.

At the time, I took that as a compliment. I am deeply ashamed of that now, and I so regret all the lunches, laughs, and sharing that I missed with my female friends in the company cafeteria. I would love the opportunity to replay that scene, but instead I will extend forgiveness to myself for my naïveté and this self-inflicted wound. I apologize to my sisters for my abandonment, and I add my promise to pay attention to all the ways we work against ourselves and help others to see this as well.

Stepping back from chronic overworking—from redefining *extraordinary* as not extra at all but just what we do all day every day—is not easy. I am trying, with very uneven success, to do it right now as I write this. At the same time that I want us all to feel included and valued, I am striving to make each word I put on paper brilliant and clever and funny so I secure my position as extraordinary in your eyes, when all I really need to do is show you this concept in a way that is understandable and accessible.

On Being Extraordinary

I have intentionally flooded these pages with the word *extraordinary* coupled with a negative charge until I have become sick of writing it and sick of thinking about it. I know that I must temper the energy I instinctively allot to this idea in order to place it in rightful balance with my well-being. It is indeed a chore, but like any new habit, it becomes easier. I do not want any of us to curtail the joyful, rewarding, truly extraordinary things that we do that resonate with who we are. In fact, those things are salve on our overworked souls. I do, however, want us to stop ourselves and each other just long enough to question whether a particular thing we are about to take on has to be extraordinary, or whether *good enough* might just be—good enough.

On Being Extraordinary

I have witnessed it,
I have mimicked it,
I profit by it—to a point:
To the point of exhaustion
All the way to resentment.
Let that not be my legacy to my daughter.
Let that go.

My grandmothers did not really have a choice other than chronic overwork, but I do. *We* do. I want all of us, our entire sisterhood, to pause and consider the choice to be extraordinary, and make it a *choice*. Let *that* be our legacy to the next generation.

Good Enough Might Just Be Good Enough

When I was studying for my master's degree in social work, I read lots of books, articles, and papers on parenting—the good, the bad, and the proverbial ugly. We had spirited debates in class about the ideal parent, or rather the ideal conditions in order to raise a child optimally.

We were assigned the reading of D.W. Winnicott, a pediatrician and psychoanalyst who coined the phrase "good enough mother." (It was 1953, so I'll forgive him for not using *parent*.) He wrote that a woman should not strive to be "perfect" or "best" (or extraordinary), as that could cause unintended consequences for both the mother and the child. He went on to say that raising a psychologically healthy child who feels "loved and nurtured" requires only that we take care of the baby's "basic physical and emotional needs." If the baby feels "overall safe and loved she will be able to tolerate and forgive [mother's] imperfections."[44]

Winnicott went on to say that "perfection isn't possible in *any* human relationship." He emphasizes to "stop thinking of motherhood as effortless all-giving because the healthiest approach preserves room for the mother's own physical, emotional, and social space."[45]

Winnicott said that a child raised to think the world is there to meet its every need is not well prepared for life. Additionally, the "perfect mother isn't a healthy model for them either, because [the mother's] so self-depriving."[46]

Accepting that good enough is good enough is a daily discipline. To this day, with my children now adults, I still struggle with this. Everything that went wrong in their lives and every disappointment they have, I can trace back to some slight in my parenting, some missed opportunity or lack of encouragement or the wrong degree of love, from unconditional fawning to boundary-setting "tough love" applied at the wrong time.

It seems how we were mothered and how we mother creates extraordinary expectations of chronic giving without regard for ourselves. *No wonder* we so often work against our own best interests!

A Letter to My Past Self

Dear Lynn,

It's 2021. I'm writing to you from your future, frankly with deep disappointment that there isn't much in common with the future I thought I (and all the budding feminists of the '60s) were fighting for. We thought we'd be handing off a much more just world to you, and certainly for your

---

44 Alexandra Sacks, "The Good Enough Mother," Medium, May 4, 2018, medium.com/@alexandrasacks/the-good-enough-mother-ab19fd7dad06.

45 Sacks.

46 Sacks.

daughters. We failed, or at least mostly failed. So let me warn you about what's ahead.

You're going to work too hard all the time. At home, at school, and in the workplace. You will be told that women can now "have it all," and in a way, that is true, but the cost is terribly high. In 2021, you will still be doing 4.5 hours of unpaid labor each day, compared to men's 1.3 hours.

Women now run for office and serve in greater numbers. In 2021, there will be a record number of women serving in Congress—27% women in the House and 24% women in the Senate—but we make up 51% of the country.[47] Men—old, white men—are still making the majority of the policy decisions for women and families.

You can be proud that medical schools and some STEM PhD programs are at or nearing 50% participation for women, and women are patenting at increasing levels, but the pipeline springs a leak at the transition from student to entrepreneur. Though women start businesses at rates higher than men, women-owned businesses receive less than 3% of venture capital investment.[48]

You will be told that women are more risk averse, as if it is a character flaw. When we look a little deeper into that statistic, we discover that women are more apt to make a career choice in the context of their family situation or based on the availability of health insurance, and thus lean toward academia instead of higher potential start-up or scale-up options.

In your early career, a senior manager of a large company will tell you and another woman on the promotion track that women cannot "have

---

47 Carrie Blazina and Drew Desilver, "A Record Number of Women Are Serving in the 117th Congress," Pew Research Center, January 15, 2021, www.pewresearch.org/fact-tank/2021/01/15/a-record-number-of-women-are-serving-in-the-117th-congress/.

48 Katherina Kuschel et al. "Stemming the Gender Gap in STEM Entrepreneurship—Insights into Women's Entrepreneurship in Science, Technology, Engineering and Mathematics," *International Entrepreneurship and Management Journal* 16 (2020): 1-15, doi.org/10.1007/s11365-020-00642-5; "35 Women-Owned Business Statistics You Need to Know in 2021"; Ashley Bittner and Brigette Lau, "Women-Led Startups Received Just 2.3% of VC Funding in 2020," Harvard Business Review, February 25, 2021, hbr.org/2021/02/women-led-startups-received-just-2-3-of-vc-funding-in-2020.

it all." Of marriage, career, and parenthood, he will say that you can have two, but not three. It turns out he was right. Parenting young children significantly lowers the probability of entrepreneurial activity for women, but there is no corresponding effect for men.[49] You will be allowed and encouraged to *do* it all, but that's not anyone's version of "*having* it all."

You will work on this issue because you care deeply about the future of women and children and families in general. You will believe you are taking up the cause in homage to your grandmothers, who were extraordinary beyond measure in order to support themselves and their families. You will call, march, write, petition your government, contact your legislators, organize protests, work on campaigns, run for office, and serve, but your outsized efforts will yield only modest results.

You will become extraordinary. You will believe that this will be an occasional sprint to accomplish a goal along the way to justice and equality. You will imagine a respite after each dash but defer it once again as there is more to do and so few who are able.

You become chronically extraordinary, and then very tired, and later full of rage and joylessness, and then exhausted, until you realize there is no rest. Our country is happy to have half its population overwork in order for others to profit. You will become dispirited and resentful. You need to be warned.

But if I tell you all of this, you may not believe me. I don't want you to believe me. I don't want to believe me. But you need to know that *every day* you will work 4.5 hours of unpaid labor on top of everything else you will be doing, and that must be accounted for in your success equation. If you try to birth a world-changing business, you are many times more likely to fail than your male counterparts. If you decide to have a child, the likelihood of even starting your business plummets. You need to be warned that if you choose two (marriage and career, parenthood and

---

[49] Margaret E. Blume-Kohout, "Understanding the Gender Gap in STEM Fields Entrepreneurship," Office of Advocacy, October 1, 2014, advocacy.sba.gov/2014/10/01/understanding-the-gender-gap-in-stem-fields-entrepreneurship/.

marriage, parenthood and career), you might be happy, but if you choose all three, you will be overworked, underappreciated, and worried about the time you spend away from your family as well as the time you spend away from your job, all while you continuously strive for a balance that is impossible to strike.

You will have to choose between being a bad mother or an average worker—or exhausting yourself to the point that your life has almost no resemblance to the vision and hope I can see in you now. You will trade burning passion for burning out, realizing too late there are no sparks left to fan into flame.

Oh, my dear Lynn, I can't tell you this. This cannot be what I pass on in my chain of extraordinary women. What then? I can only warn you to get off this path if I can point you to another. Another path that is smoother, where there is compassion and support and laughter. Where you will be healthy and helpful, committed and supported. Where you will use your power intentionally at the center of its warmth and comfort. Where you will be part of a sisterhood that knows everything you need to know and shares everything that needs to be shared—burdens and joys, tricks and hacks, and a map showing the alligators in the pond.

We will all learn together how to, as Meg Conley (who you will meet in your future) says, "stop reaching up and instead reach out" so that we all get there together.[50]

I wish I'd written sooner.

Love,
Lynn

---

50 Conley, "Motherhood in America Is a Multilevel Marketing Scheme."

Chapter 5

Reach Out, Not Up!

What is the alternative to this toxic culture of extraordinary-ism we swim in?

I do not dispute the value of realigning one's mindset, as that is part of what I will describe in the next chapters, but I want to be resolute in the assertion that changing one's mindset alone cannot change a system that is not rigged in our favor. It is past time that we reject "We can do it!" as a success strategy, and discarding it must come first in the form of changing our behavior.

Give Us a Break

Our first priority in getting on this new path is to give ourselves a big fucking break *every day*.

Reminding ourselves that we mostly succeed "in spite of" instead of "because of" is a good place to start. It is critical to begin with ourselves. We need to have ample empathy and forgiveness for ourselves before it can spill over to others. We need to believe in our bones that what we do every day is good enough—and most days so much more than that—and that the answer to the disarray and difficulties in our lives is not to do more.

Our second priority in getting on a new path is to give *each other* a break—yes, a big fucking break. There are attitudes and national policies to change before relief will be in sight, but in the meantime, while we work or wait for change, we must first acknowledge our outsized role in the world. Say to each other: "*No wonder* we are exhausted! Let us give ourselves a break. There you are. I see you. I see what you are doing, what you don't have time to do, and I see how amazing the outcome of your efforts is."

Giving ourselves and each other a break is the first step toward acknowledging the bind we're in and supporting each other to get out of it. Giving ourselves and each other a break is about developing and expressing empathy.

Remember Meg Conley, who so articulately laid out the undervaluing of women's work in Chapter 2? She sees this bind and cautions us: "We shouldn't be trying to reach the top; we should be trying to reach each other."[51]

So, let us look at some tools for reaching toward each other.

EMPATHY ON THE FLY

Thinking back to my grandmothers and how isolated and alone they were makes me want to imagine them on a new path with us. Instead of being rejected by men and shunned by women for choosing to support their families when their husbands could not or would not, what if a circle of sisters had dropped off an occasional meal, offered a ride to work when the car was in the garage, taken care of some after-school child-minding, or even asked the occasional "How do you do it all?" What if they had a sisterhood as a buffer to their isolation?

When I first began thinking about this book and how to share the magic of a sisterhood, I initially called what I am about to describe "episodic lateral mentoring." I thought that if I was writing a book, I ought to give the catalyst for said magic a name worthy of its weight and impact. Actually, my first try at naming it was "episodic nonhierarchical mentoring."

So, what exactly is that? It is not sitting at the master's hem. It is not the master-and-apprentice male model of mentoring where, in a rigid hierarchy, one teaches and the other learns. It is instead simple. What I

---

51   Conley, "Motherhood in America Is a Multilevel Marketing Scheme."

am really talking about is empathy. Empathy that is completely authentic, offered and accepted by equals— often on the fly. It communicates "I see you, I get it, I've been there, you're doing just fine."

Referring back to the repeating E-Cycle,™ we routinely perform at an extraordinary level, we exhaust ourselves in this unsustainable pace, and we look to the promise of some sort of empowerment as a solution or even respite. We are desperate and vulnerable to the myth that individual behaviors and actions can bring us power to better regulate our lives. We take the course, buy the book, and get up an hour earlier, further encumbering ourselves by adding another set of to-dos to our already too long list. And repeat.

But what if we insert empathy in a few key places in this cycle, first for ourselves and then for one another? Empathy is an antidote to being caught in the cycle of extraordinary-ism. Empathy slows it down and allows us to become aware of our own and others' hamster wheels.

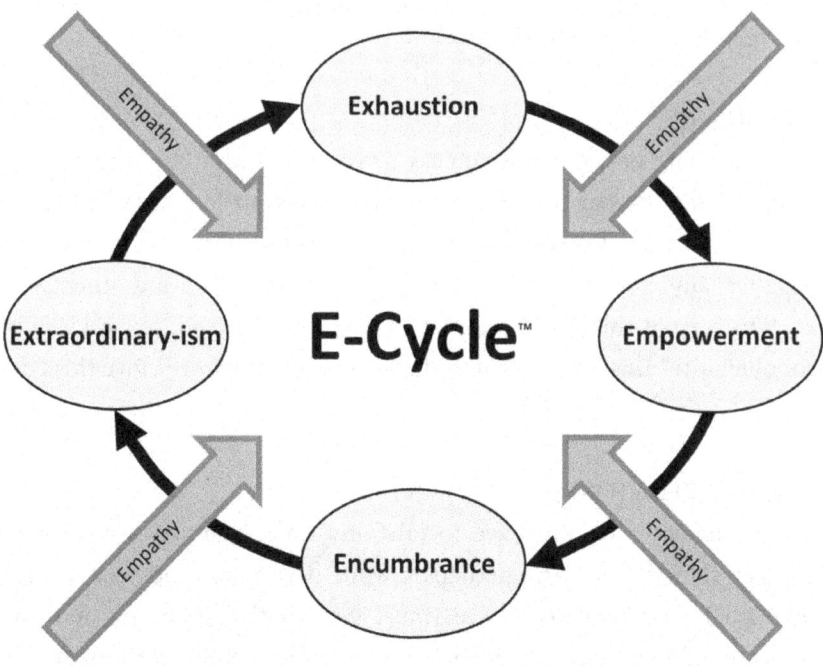

When we are overworking, before *exhaustion* overtakes, insert empathy. What if we said to ourselves: "Look what I can do even with an added 21.5 hours of unpaid labor this week?" instead of focusing on the many things remaining on our checklist for the day?

When we do get to exhaustion, well before we further *encumber* ourselves, insert empathy. What if we simply said to ourselves: "*No wonder* I'm exhausted!"?

When we circle back around to *extraordinary*, as we of course will, insert empathy again as we ask ourselves how we can do this task "well enough" while taking care of ourselves in the way we would want our loved ones to take care of themselves. What if?

Tools on the Path of Empathy

Like many paths that are not well trodden, there are bumps and undergrowth and even places where the trail disappears on the way to empathy, and we have to guess which way to go. Luckily, there are a few basic tools that help to negotiate this journey.

Language

Become aware of the words you say to yourself and others and begin to change them. Be curious and aware of where your language hurts, marginalizes, or demeans yourself or others. Be especially careful not to turn negative language on yourself that you would not use toward others, such as, "I'm crap at this" or "I look fat in this top." Instead, make kindness your default: "This isn't my strength, but I'm learning" or "I love this color on me."

Micro-behaviors

Micro-behaviors do not have to take any time. Start with quality eye contact, then a smile and perhaps a word. These are quick connections, nonverbal shorthand for "I see you; I get what's happening here, and you're not alone." These micro-behaviors are the entrance to "empathy on the fly." They can be given and received in a couple of seconds and allow you to experience the delicious effect of seeing as you extend the experience of being seen.

Recently, on one of my dreaded but necessary grocery store excursions, I found myself standing mindlessly in front of the meat case, waiting for a download of inspiration to help me decide what to get and what to do with it. There was a woman standing nearby seemingly doing the same thing. I turned to her and said, "I wish there was some new kind of meat, some new species or something. I'm so sick of looking at the same stuff, cooking the same stuff, and I'm even tired of eating the same stuff."

"I know!" she responded. We both laughed. I grabbed my usual pork tenderloin, and she asked me how I cook it. She took a package of turkey sausage and told me how she mixes it with eggs and whatever vegetables she has hanging around and bakes it into a quiche dish. I left the meat case with a lightness from the uplift one gets from being seen and recognized, *and* a new idea for an easy meal. As we encountered one another going up and down the rest of the aisles of the supermarket, we smiled in recognition each time. We did not exchange names; we did not know anything about one another save for our shared frustration with the drudgery of constant meal planning. I so love these sorts of exchanges with my sister women. They are joyous, delightful, and effective in the way they point us to another path.

EMPATHY AS AN INTENTION

As we grow our habit of empathy on the fly, we can be more conscious about extending intentional empathy as our default way of interacting with women. The key to successfully using this tool is to extend it to *all* women. This is not to say that you should be a constant empathy emanator but that when you see an opportunity for a micro-communication, do not spend a second trying to decide if this *particular* woman is worthy of it. Just *do* it as a gift to the sisterhood—to the collective—with no immediate quid pro quo expectation.

This is the stuff that you can dish out and accept daily. Some days I gain more from being on the giving end of this, and other days more from being on the receiving end. In either event, it reminds me every day that there are women struggling unseen and unappreciated everywhere. I am often one of those women, and simply being seen can be just what I need to get through a difficult moment with grace, to get through that moment without adding guilt or blame or, worse, shame to my current difficulty. Who but another woman with empathy on the fly would see you alone, nervously awaiting a cab, and stop to casually start up a conversation with you until the cab comes and she says, "Oh, your ride's here," and then waves good-bye? The common discomfort of waiting alone for a cab was so easily averted with an "I see you" act of kindness—an act of sisterhood.

As well as exploring lovely examples of intentional empathy, we can also look at missed (possibly familiar) opportunities to extend it.

Not long ago, I was driving down a divided highway, the sort with a breakdown lane where you could pull over if you had engine trouble and wait for/hope for the best. I saw this beat-up, ramshackle black car covered in bumper stickers (let's just say they were not bumper stickers that would ever appear on my car) merging onto the highway and cutting me off as she passed me on the right to get ahead of me.

As she passed, I noticed the woman looked a bit on the rough side. Her window was down, and I got a glimpse of a tattooed arm and long, bright blue painted nails as she flicked the ashes from her cigarette. Her long, permed hair was piled on top of her head, and she was talking forcefully to two children in the back seat. I downloaded a persona of her and randomly assigned her to the "not worthy of my attention" category.

Her car started to sputter a bit and slow down. As she put on her blinker and pulled into the breakdown lane, I drove by. I would like to say I thought of pulling over to see if she needed help, but it didn't occur to me until a couple of miles down the road. What would it have taken for me to simply stop and ask if she needed me to call someone or to park behind her with my flashers on until she figured out what to do? No matter what her story was or how she did or did not align with my values, she deserved to be seen. She deserved on-the-fly empathy.

GIVING AND RECEIVING: EMPATHY BEGETS EMPATHY

On a recent five-hour flight, I was seated across the aisle from a woman and her two daughters, ages four and eight, and in front of a couple with a several-month-old baby. The baby was quiet the entire time save for take-off and landing, and the girls across the aisle mostly so as their mother busied herself with dispensing well-timed snacks, reading to them, and giving them lots of screen time with their individual iPads.

As we all stood to deplane, I remarked to the woman across from me (mostly to the mom) what good travelers her girls were and how well they had managed on such a long flight.

She replied, "Oh, thank you. I worry about how much screen time I let them have. I feel a bit guilty about it, but I don't want them to disturb other passengers."

I replied, "If I'd had that option when my children were little, I would've probably let them have it for the entire trip!"

I liked that I could reply with a judgment-free observation, knowing well the guilt she described.

She said, "I can't imagine how you managed without screens. It must've been exhausting to keep ahead of them."

"It was indeed," I answered.

It was such a brief but warm and empathic conversation. We could both so easily see what was invisible to most. We could see what the other was doing or had done—being hypervigilant in order to anticipate our children's wants or needs and at the ready with whatever that might be. We saw and recognized the extraordinary care that one another gave.

We both turned to the mother behind us carrying the just-now waking baby. I noted how quiet things had been and that I had forgotten there was a baby back there. The obviously tired mom said, "He nursed and slept and nursed and slept, and now he's awake and wants to play, and I'm a tired, sweaty mess!"

"You look great," I added. "Next time, when he's older, don't forget the screens. Maybe you'll even get a nap!"

She laughed.

While her husband grabbed their luggage from above, the other mom said, "Here, let my daughter carry your diaper bag for you."

The new mother handed over the bag. We all smiled and left the plane in a bubble of empathy, three sister mothers who collided on a plane with a common experience that transcended time. It was delicious and effective.

Whether to answer a call to empathy is a choice I make each time, considering the circumstances. But the muscle I want to develop is to hear the call and see an opportunity *every time* one is presented. Micro-behaviors get you started, and an awareness of language is essential in the process, but to go through life with empathy as an intention is a change in perspective—a realignment followed by an action.

Realigning Your Mindset

Realigning one's mindset is not so much a skill or activity as it is a discipline. It falls into one of those "easier said than done" categories and thus requires commitment and recommitment. I imagine that one day, it might simply be a new habit that has become my default. I hope so, but I am not there yet. Realigning one's mindset is even more than an intention. It is a decision that one must make every day.

Decision versus Reaction

Nanny B. did not like cursing. Meanwhile, my language of annoyance is particularly salty. I often think of it as a natural, authentic, reaction, not a decision. But I am wrong. Nanny B. would explain to me that people who curse are trying to express themselves as best they can but that their "limited vocabulary" is the reason they curse. As I would never want to be tagged with that description, I would take care to say things like "Susie is exasperating," or "My father was profoundly attached to an opinion that he considered a fact." It was my decision to describe my feelings and mood (in the presence of my grandmother) in words— as is my decision to curse loudly.

I am often annoyed with the many insults and failures of grace and ease that any ordinary day can bring: the car in front of me that is going too slowly, the waitstaff who misses that I was next in line, a loved one who forgets something important to me, or even the drawbridge going up when I am late. I can—and too often do—use these examples as confirmation that the world is a cold and uncaring place. Or I can ask myself how many annoying things are happening and how am I managing my mood. Even better, I might (on a really good day) be able to extend empathy to those who are disappointing me as well as to myself for deciding on annoyance as my mood for the day.

When I imagine the driver of the slow car has just received some bad news, remember that the loved one who forgets is still a loved one in my midst, or tell myself the waitstaff is working as fast as possible and is distracted as anyone would be, my mood regulates a bit.

Make a decision to challenge your mood. Require more evidence that the day is indeed a bad one.

When explaining the concept of this book to my writing coach and describing how we can decide to challenge ourselves or accept our usual responses, she told me this story:

> "My own experience of the sisterhood happened one evening when I went to the local frozen yogurt shop I frequent for my usual favorite dessert. I recognized the girl behind the counter, whom I had seen the last few times there but had never spoken to beyond giving my order and saying the cursory 'please' and 'thank you' that came with being a customer. But this time, something was different.

"I saw her as a sister instead of just someone behind the counter taking my order. I decided to strike up a conversation and asked her how she liked working there, what it was like, and where she had worked before. It was actually a really lovely moment of connection where I felt like we shared a moment of understanding. When I left, I felt uplifted, and I knew she felt seen. The most amazing part is that, for the first time, I realized we shared an unspoken connection. We both had the same name. We were both Ashley."

Cultivate an Aspiration to Be Merely Competent

Each of us has our own list of mindset downloads that do not serve us and could use realignment. Make your own list and invite yourself and others to challenge them. But also let me draw your attention to one that is endemic to women and propose that we challenge it daily as part of our collective responsibility to the sisterhood.

Realign Your Mindset About Competence

Trade your expectation of always being *excellent* to *good enough* as often as you can. And market it to other women.

- The sink was full of dishes when you left for work. YEA!
- Your kids will have to eat school lunch because you are not packing lunches today. YEA!
- The meeting minutes have only the most important things, not everything. If you forget something, that is what the "Any additions or corrections?" question is for! YEA!
- When you inevitably show up late to something because you were [fill in the blank: dropping something off, picking something up, waiting for the cable guy to show up], do not apologize or even explain your good excuse because we all know you have one. Say instead, "Please excuse me for being unavoidably late. I'll catch up on what I missed with one of you." YEA!

This is actually a fun icebreaker exercise. We can call it "Cards Against Extraordinary-ism" inspired by the crass, raunchy, and "more fun than it ought to be" Cards Against Humanity game. Make a list of extraordinary behaviors familiar to us all and fill in the blanks with what you would rather do. Make the answers fun and outrageous. Instead of the extraordinary choice, come up with an ordinary alternative. For instance:

Extraordinary Choice	Ordinary Alternative
Of course, I'll work overtime to get this done.	If this can't be done during my workday, then I'm *way* underpaid.
I can make the cake topper animals out of fondant and the barn out of LEGO bricks.	Will you pick up a cake at the grocery store on the way home? Oh yeah, and have them write "Happy Birthday" on top.
Can you take over the management of this project? You've got the best handle on it. It shouldn't be any additional time. Sure, I can do it more easily than Joe can.	Happy to rewrite the contract and add project management to the strategy and consultation currently being provided.
Company is coming! Vacuum, dust, put the pile of unopened mail out of sight, search Pinterest for unique and delicious meals, and get a special bottle of wine.	Clean the toilet, wipe out the sink, serve an old favorite or get some takeout. Bonus points for adding: "I'm having you here for dinner as the dust isn't as visible in the evening hours. It's pretty scary around here in full sunlight."
Can you stop by the vet's on your way home from work to pick up the special food for Fido? Of course!	Not today. That dog eats better than I do. I'm going to stop and get some high-quality takeout. Special food for humans!

You get the idea. Have fun with it and let me know what you come up with!

The mutual benefits will be immediate when we extend empathy on the fly to our sisters and ourselves. We will often feel a lightheartedness and even find humor in our shared experience, which will give us access to an additional menu of thought, creativity, and action.

While I find rage and anger painful and immobilizing in isolation, it can shift to annoyance and alternate action when I open the window to empathy in connection with another. Sisterhood as transformation is exquisite on an individual level. Contemplating sisterhood as a group strategy to bend the system in our favor is as stunning in its effect as it is in its simplicity.

The way to unencumber ourselves is to stop the endless climb toward "success" and start climbing toward each other. Women have the ability to nurture each other in deep and magical ways. It is a secret superpower—the best life hack you will ever find. It is revolutionary and countercultural in all the best ways.

CHAPTER 6

Fight Invisibility

Women are invisible in so many ways. We have all experienced the interpersonal invisibility of being spoken over or marginalized or discounted. There are so many examples in our daily lives that are collectively overwhelming, a constant reminder that we were not expected in the world of work and certainly not anticipated.

We are invisible in product design, making our experience of invisibility visceral and constant: the seat belt that crosses our bodies at the neck unless we are over five feet six, unreachable kitchen shelves, cell phones too big for our hands, no place for a purse or bag in our cars (you can't even get a purse place option, but you can get a gun rack!), no room to nurse at work, National Institutes of Health studies on heart disease incorrectly thinking it was a man's disease for decades and not including women in the studies, and on and on.[52]

As a partial antidote to invisibility, we want to be certain that women are not invisible to one another. This begins with our intention to notice, to see others, and to assume we are worthy of the same. With choosing to be sisters individually and collectively.

It is simple to get started, but it is not easy.

Though there are techniques like the Six Cs and other guidelines described later in this book, the primary ingredient for taking on women's

---

52 Caroline Criado Perez, *Invisible Women: Data Bias in a World Designed for Men* (New York: Abrams, 2019).

invisibility is your own desire for a different way. Whether you have come to this topic because of frustration, exhaustion, skepticism, or a sense of "why bother" hopelessness, congratulations—you are on the path.

This path will lead you to see and be seen by your sisters. It will help you desert *extraordinary-ism* and false *empowerment*, and find the road less traveled: sanity born of sisterhood. But sisterhood goes against the status quo; you will need to be willing to step up and act outside of society's norms.

BE WILLING TO DEFY THE NORM

If you are still reading, you are likely ready for the critical next step. You must cross the boundary of what is expected, of what is the norm. And yes, challenging norms is yet another activity on our proverbial to-do lists. The fresh air brought by defying the status quo is almost immediate. Once a norm is challenged, a boundary crossed, there is no need to go back. Those on either side of the boundary can feel the difference and experience the result that unfolds.

THE SCARF

Once when I was shopping with my infant and my shirt was suddenly wet with milk from my overfull breasts, an unknown woman silently placed her scarf around my neck and whispered, "Keep it." She crossed such a boundary. She saw my dilemma and chose to offer a solution, unsolicited. She touched me, she spoke to me, and she gifted me her scarf. Her on-the-fly empathy transformed me from a harried, unprepared, sloppy, and embarrassed new mother to a sister—a nursing mother with an abundance of milk to nourish my child and who happened to have a wet shirt *and* a lovely scarf to cover it.

I felt immediately recognized, valued, worthy of help, and completely unencumbered of embarrassment and shame. When she took that step toward the sisterhood path, she not only showed me the benefit of it, but she also presented me with the entrance to that very path, and once seen, it could not be unseen. We exchanged only quick smiles and eye contact, but she remains one of my original sisters. I kept the scarf as a cherished talisman of sisterhood, often putting it over my shoulders as I nursed. Long after I had put it away in a drawer, I could still smell the woman's perfume. It was Joy. Of course it was.

Women exist in an environment and an economy that was not rigged for us, nor has it been sufficiently amended to properly accommodate us. Many of the boundaries that keep us disconnected serve the constructs that impede our success.

Think about the taboo of talking salary with one's co-workers. Whom does this serve? I can recall getting a raise and being told not to "tell the other girls" because they weren't getting the level of pay that I was. Sadly, I did what was expected; I did not challenge that norm or push that boundary. This feigned confidence on the part of the company served the purpose of making me feel special and valued—and also to separate me from the other women in my office.

I did not cross the normative boundary that discouraged sisterhood. In my defense, at the time I could not have imagined another path. Nonetheless, I still feel the pang of regret when I think of how I was complicit with the status quo of paying women less than their actual value.

THE COURAGE TO STEP ONTO THE PATH

Before we connect in a sisterhood and start down a barely trodden, near-invisible, usually prohibited, sometimes dangerous path, we must make an internal decision to be uncomfortable.

I recently read in an article on the popular "Scary Mommy" blog about mothers returning to work and the importance of having uncomfortable conversations, particularly if one had stepped out of the workforce for a while.

One such woman asked a group of colleagues what they were being paid and discovered that one of the men was paid a full $10,000 a year more than she was to do the same work. In her example, she expressed gratitude for the man who shared his salary information and noted that he offered to coach her on how to ask for more money.

This example of a woman willing to challenge the norm by asking about salary points out the initial decision and how it enables a first step on a new path. This is a critical step, which takes courage and intention. There is no guarantee that it will result in a positive change, but there is a guarantee that, once crossed, this boundary is forever permeable.

Thinking systemically, the thoughtful and generous reaction of her colleague offers the benefit of concrete data and the suggestion of an action, but it addresses the pay inequity injustice for only one person. When we enlarge the conversation with more *communication*, *cooperation*, and—hopefully—*collaboration*, we can then ask as a group (a sisterhood): "Are men and women paid equitably in this company, and if not, what can we do about it?" It is then that we make the path more obvious—wider—and we begin to smooth it out for our sisters to follow and to invite others in.

BEING SEEN, DEFINED

Being seen often gets described incorrectly as wanting acknowledgment. It demeans this important element by reducing it to women needing to be thanked for what we do. Being acknowledged and thanked is lovely, but it is not the equivalent of being seen. An "OK, thanks for reminding me to pick up Johnny at soccer," or "Thanks for catching the typo in my report," or "Thanks for doing the prep work for the meeting that went so smoothly" is certainly a lovely acknowledgment, but being seen is so much more than that.

We all love to be thanked, but we aspire to be visible and be considered in the making of policy and design, whether it be in relation to maternity leave, workstations, healthcare, pockets in clothing, or the location of women's restrooms. We are invisible when policy or designs are made for us without us.

During the height of the COVID-19 lockdown, most children received some or all of their schooling at home via the internet. Women were simply assumed and tacitly drafted to the duty of enabling and supervising this activity. The actual impact this would have on the lives of women was barely considered. Women were invisible. We were not seen, and we were not acknowledged. The disproportionate impact of this responsibility for homeschooling with assumed, volunteer, unpaid staffing by women continues to resonate in the negative and disproportionate impact it has had on women's jobs and careers.[53] Perhaps to hammer the point home, imagine sending women off to staff COVID testing centers or do contact tracing with the assumption that men would pick up the homeschooling and additional household responsibility!

The Power of an Eye Roll, Real or Symbolic

Women are generally not invisible to other women. We can communicate in shorthand in a way that is efficient and affirming. When we encounter a mother with a toddler having a tantrum, a smile and an eye roll lets her know we get it—we have been there (or we are glad we are not there now). When a woman in a meeting is interrupted or spoken over, or her point repeated or "explained" by a man, we can say something on her behalf. If that is not possible, we can be sure to meet her eyes and let her know we saw it. We know what it is, and she is not invisible to us.

There is immense relief in being seen. My anger and frustration at being invisible can be very toxic. It can stick with me for hours or even days, probably longer, and it can be cumulative.

Conversely, when I am met with acknowledgment, an eye roll, a smile, or a smirk, I can fairly easily let it go. I do not mean let go of the issue or give in to the inequity but let go of the resentment and frustration surrounding it. Being alone with resentment and frustration is a pretty straight road to exhaustion and—sometimes—depression for me. The acknowledgment from a sister—the acknowledgment that I am not

---

[53] Nicole Bateman and Martha Ross, "Why Has COVID-19 Been Especially Harmful for Working Women?," Brookings, October 14, 2020, www.brookings.edu/essay/why-has-covid-19-been-especially-harmful-for-working-women/.

invisible—assures me that I am not alone and is a very effective antidote to the slippery slope of toxic negativity and disease.

Like many women, the lives of my foremothers were difficult, as has been mine at times. For me, it was made more so by my response to the difficulty—the loneliness of feeling different and my very real sense of isolation. I do not experience that any longer. Well, that is not exactly right. Sometimes it returns, but it does not stick. When I feel the old, familiar toxic responses rising, I trust my antidote: a sister or a sisterhood. It is impossible to believe negative self-talk in the face of my sisters. Sometimes I do not even need to actually talk with them, but simply imagine what they might say or how they might laugh or roll their eyes.

Being Seen

This evolution from invisibility to being seen is the debt we pay our foremothers. It is the debt we pay forward to remind every woman to ignore the dangerous myth of empowerment. To remind every woman that the exhausting to-do list of standing straight, leaning in, speaking up, or washing one's face will not change a system rigged against us. Instead, we will trade our exhaustion for the path of sisterhood, a path that, walked together, is joyous, delightful, and effective.

For most of my life and all of my career, I have been, as Gina Glantz calls it, a gender avenger:[54] an activist, an evangelist, and a radical impatiently advocating for and often demanding the equity and justice that women are yet to fully experience. Gains have been made—impressive gains. Yet, at the same time, it is astonishing and profoundly disappointing that in the twenty-first century, when women hold the majority in the population, we are still largely invisible in policy and design and remain a stubborn minority in places of power and influence.

This struggle for equity, justice, a good job with good pay and recognition, affordable childcare, accessible healthcare, and more has led, in great part, to my sense of exhaustion and my push toward chronic

---

54 A term she even harnessed to create a nonprofit: www.genderavenger.com/.

extraordinary-ism. But as I contemplate the sisterhood that I describe here and advocate for us all, it is only now that I understand the flaw in my binary thinking and doing.

Give in or fight like hell, go along or stand out, agree or disagree, conform or be alone— these were the choices I thought were available to me. "If you're not a part of the solution, you're a part of the problem" has a ring of truth in it, but it misses the critical point: How do we live a joyous life on the way to justice?

We become visible. Visible to our sisters, visible to ourselves, and through that, visible to the world.

Chapter 7

The Magic of the Group Effect

We begin with the understanding that the system is not rigged in our favor, that much, if not most, is designed without giving even a thought to "How might this work for women?" Once the system's impact is understood, we can challenge the assumption that we should be chronically *extraordinary*, and we can give ourselves that big fucking break. Then we can turn to the bushwhacking that reveals the path that we all can take, extending this same break to all women, to our sisters. "Reach out, not up." Connect rather than climb. Nourish each other rather than choosing to stay on the treadmill designed to wear us out without lifting us up.

We talked about some general ways in which to gain that mindset, but now let's turn toward a much more specific tool to not only nourish each other, but to lift each other toward the success we desire in a more humane and holistic way: the magic of groups.

My First Experience with the Magic of Sisterhood in a Group

The formula for success, discovered in retrospect, is simple: six C words. Verbs. *Collide, communicate, connect, cooperate, collaborate,* and when necessary, *collude.* We can use them individually every day in couplets or triplets. When we move from empathy on the fly to operationalizing these words for a concrete purpose, we use them all in sequence, in a community of sisterhood. And we make magic.

There is an important, beautiful story I want to tell you. It is the punch line, or better said, the *payoff* of this path I am sketching. I am tempted to build up the suspense and anticipation and give you this precious story at the end. But instead, I will tell this story backwards, which is the way I learned it. I learned it after *colliding* with six other women—"the Seven Sisters," as we began to call ourselves—during the subconscious forming of our group, our sisterhood community.

We all worked in the Obama administration as small-business advocates, each with our own region and each trusted to use our skills and networks in our own particular way to do our work. There were ten of us; seven of us were women. Our boss was gifted in the way that excellent managers are. His leadership looked effortless. The effect was high productivity, high morale, and mutual respect.

It was important to him that we felt we were a team, even though we were far-flung across the country, from Seattle to New Orleans, California to Maine, and all the places in between. We gathered together in Washington, D.C. regularly and had a weekly phone call we all attended. We also shared our weekly reports with one another. When we came to Washington, there was a nice mix of programming, business, and social time. Some of it was lightly structured, but most of it was not, and it was not long before the seven women started to gravitate toward each other. We began to *communicate*. We all spoke of how unique it was that out of the ten of us, we had a female majority. In fact, we jokingly appointed one of our male colleagues the head of what we deemed the "men's minority caucus."

Our sister group *connected*—tentatively at first—but later, when we were overtly and intentionally *cooperating*, we began to openly discuss how much we enjoyed this particular group of women and how easy and pleasant it was to work together. At the same time, we did not all *like* each other at first, and if I were to choose a group of women to work with, this was not the group I would have curated. Of the six others, there was one I immediately liked, one I did not, and one I found annoying. The rest did not initially register one way or the other. This turned out to be completely irrelevant to our sisterhood.

I respected all of these women for the skills and experience they had and the networks they created. Each of us approached our work in very different ways, and we were generous with our ideas, knowledge, and work methods. Sometime around the beginning of our second year together, we developed a common language about this being the best job we had ever had.

We credited our boss for his high expectations, his affirmative support, and perhaps most of all, his assumption that we knew how to do what we knew how to do and trusted us to do it and support each other in it. But, in retrospect, it was the sisterhood that most defined this job as our best ever.

We seven women, who otherwise would never have come to know each other, became the self-appointed Seven Sisters, a random group with nothing obvious in common except our job—well, that and our political party. After initially *colliding* and *connecting*, we frequently *communicated*. Given any opportunity, we always *cooperated*. And later, we *collaborated*.

We would see a need or a direction we wanted the office to focus on, talk about it together, and then suggest it to our immediate boss and send it up the line. One of our favorite projects was the Innovation Initiative that we worked on together. We were all advocates for the small businesses in our various regions across the country. This primarily involved working with businesses to assess the likely impact of pending regulation, and then working to intervene in said regulation when it was expected to land disproportionately hard on small business. Where this was most prominent and problematic was with startup and innovative types of businesses, as existing regulatory structures could not easily anticipate the challenges or even the business models of emerging industry.

Several of us had specific experience in this space, and all of us were interested in using our position and perspective to look for what one of the Sisters called "barriers, best practices, and big ideas" to better support innovation and entrepreneurship, as it was a priority of the administration. The idea for a specific focus on innovation bubbled up from our interest, took shape as we Seven Sisters discussed it together, and was endorsed, adopted, and promoted by our boss.

As the administration was winding down, we began to think about what our next steps would be. Even if the same party stayed in power after an election, all the political appointees would resign in order for the new government to assemble its own team. We Seven Sisters started to communicate about how we would go about finding our next great job, business, or cause. We often spoke of the effectiveness of the "good ol' boy" network and how it was not an option for us. We all had stories of how we had been passed over for younger, inexperienced men, and even men of the other party. Despite our many collective years of public service, the experience of a network looking out for us and assuming we would want or need help was foreign to us.

Thus the "good ol' girls" network was born. Actually, that name lasted for only a few minutes. We were not replicating a network that was not welcoming to us; we were simply taking our sisterhood to its next logical step. We began to *collaborate* (and yes, there was a bit of collusion) on a project to help ourselves and each other find our next steps.

We met for dinner in a lovely outdoor restaurant where the vibe was very laid back and we did not feel hurried. We had dinner, and as we lingered over dessert, we began our process. One of us agreed to take notes, and we started to go around the circle each answering the question, "What do you want to do?" or "What are you looking for?"

At this very moment, I can still feel the anxiety that question creates for me. It did then and it does now. I did not plan my career. I just took it as it came, picking up options that interested me, challenges that excited me, or opportunities that fit the flexibility I needed when I had a family. I'm a generalist, so I don't have a title like stockbroker, lawyer, or teacher. I majored in English. I have no MBA or any other obvious qualifier for me to have an opinion about business strategy. I used to think that was a huge impediment. I remember almost always feeling capable but not qualified: able to do the job, but not able to prove that I could.

This exercise got us nowhere, really. I don't remember any of us listing a particular job or even describing the sort of work we wanted to do. I started having this sinking feeling that our previous job—the best job I had ever had, where we did good work, got great reviews, and had such a wonderful experience being colleagues—was just a fluke. Maybe it was a one-off I had stumbled into and just happened to have done well. It was probably a one-time event, the high point of my career. All this doubt came because I did not have a name for all that I had done and all that I would do in my next job.

One of the sisters said, "This isn't really helping. Why don't we back up and go around the table and tell each one what they do the best and what we count on them for."

So, we all took turns telling the spotlighted woman what she did well and how we counted on her. We moved to the next woman and the next until we had finished. Each of us had a different set of skills and values that the others noted and appreciated, but *not one* of us had counted those things as an important part of our qualifications. I didn't even realize the things that people counted on from me (quick assessment, ability to synthesize and summarize and to leverage a relevant network) were even that big of a deal because they came so easily to me. All of us had the same experience. The traits and skills and values that were noted and most admired were ones that came to us naturally, almost like breathing. Since they were easy, we did not put much value on them. This was the universal response to the exercise.

By the end, each of us was in tears, as we had never heard these things articulated. We did not even really know them ourselves. This is part of the magic of sisterhood, and once experienced, once tasted and tested, I wanted more. I wanted to have more and to be a part of creating more. We all did.

The C-Words Explored
Let's delve into each C-word so you get a sense of where the magic comes from. We will talk more about the how-to details later.

Collide
Before you can have a group effect, you must first have a group.

Whenever two gather, we can be sisters; with three or more, a sisterhood. The key here is to use whatever grouping of women comes together naturally in your life. It is critical that the forming of the group is relatively random but intentional. Every book we read about mentorship and support or sponsorship urges us to choose carefully, picking someone we admire or someone who has a position to help us up the ladder. But it is important not to start recruiting women for their particular skills and sensibilities or because they are well-positioned in their lives or careers. Resist this urge—and it is an urge. Take the serendipitous nature of the collide seriously.

Focus on the groups close at hand. Perhaps it is a group of women you eat with at work, or meet on a playground while their children play, or at a food bank where you pick up food for the week, or where you might volunteer. Maybe it is women you see while waiting for your train or bus, or women who get off each day at your stop, or the other moms who are waiting with you to drop off their children at school. At that moment when the kids have hopped on the bus, or you and your bus mates come to your stop, before you go home to what awaits—back to your paid or unpaid work, or to your endless errands or the calls you will make—you are a group of sisters with a common experience that has sisterhood community potential.

Communicate
Moving from colliding to intentionally communicating is the step that stops most of us. And I can tell you that our reluctance, or the reasons for it, are surprisingly similar:

- We're not really friends.

- I forgot their names, or even better, I've been encountering them for years, and I never asked their name.

- They all seem to know each other, but they don't know me.

- I'm new. Maybe this is presumptuous.

- Everyone is too busy.

- I'm not important or worthy of their time or thought or generosity. (Ouch.)

When you are able to push past your reluctance, say something that describes what you are doing, feeling, thinking, or needing. Something that you suspect others might be feeling or doing, or a question they might answer. Something like asking for recommendations for a gynecologist or a place to get a haircut. Perhaps dare to hint at a bigger conversation like "Is anybody job hunting or trying to figure out how to do that?"

You have now officially set up the circumstances that will lead to what is next: *connection*.

This behavior is uncomfortable for most of us and can feel risky. It might be met with reluctance or silence, or you might even get a flat "No, not interested," or more likely, "No, too busy," but I doubt it. In fact, if you do get that answer, I would like to hear about it.

This is a big step, so give yourself permission to be clumsy or reluctant or even to have a few false starts before you jump in. Remember, you know something the rest of the group wants to know, and you are the spark.

CONNECT

The actual moment of connection is hard to spot and difficult to create on purpose. It is a subtle yet strong sort of energy that is as unmistakable as it is indescribable. It starts to happen on its own. Then, it is up to us to nurture it, blowing gently on the spark until it is set aflame all on its own.

When that happens, all the rest becomes possible.

For the Seven Sisters, it began with a couple of us arranging to stay at the same hotel, then adding others. We would walk to the office or cab together. During our workday, we had various meetings, briefings, and discussions that included most of the office—women and men. But at the end of the day, we seven (or sometimes five or six, whoever could make it) would intentionally get together for a meal or a drink and some conversation. We had not named our group, and we had not adopted any purpose or agenda; we simply had a tacit agreement that we enjoyed this group.

As soon as someone said, "I really like this group of seven women," we all recognized that we were indeed a "a thing," but little did we know how critical that particular moment of *connection* was. We had our first universal agreement: We liked the discussions and camaraderie that we were creating.

COOPERATE

This is probably the easiest of the C-words. In fact, I think many groups that have sisterhood potential can get stalled here by trying to be too much or too little. Cooperating is finding mutual convenience; it is not a deep connection or purposeful action. When we begin to *cooperate*, we make small agreements: "Shall we meet at the playground on Tuesday?"; "I'll pay for the cab on the way to the office, and you can get it on the way back"; "I forgot my charger, may I use yours?"

Loftier goals must wait until there is an affirmative agreement for the group to function in a particular way—as a group. It is easy for individuals within the group to cooperate with one another; it is another matter to assume agreement before it has been decided and voiced that the group will form a vehicle for concrete purposes, that the members will be part of a group *collaboration*.

COLLABORATE

The difference between cooperate and collaborate is subtle but critical. When we cooperate or collaborate, we work together for a common goal or outcome. But what turns cooperation into collaboration is the "nuance which is shared identity over individual identity. In cooperation it is vice versa. Individuality over shared identity."[55]

Think of a potluck dinner where we meet at one location and each of us brings something to share. Someone might say, "This dessert is fabulous. Can you share the recipe?" That's an example of *cooperation*.

Collaboration demands a bit more, a subtle acknowledgment of where we sit in the whole context. Instead of just a potluck dinner, we might decide on a Mexican theme and perhaps assign or each offer to bring a different course. Collaboration begins with a perspective of shared identity. It might sound like, "I love these sisterhood potluck dinners. The food is always great. How shall we do the next one?"

The key in this sort of collaboration is mutuality—that all are considered equal in status and importance. I wanted to call this peer mentoring, then lateral mentoring, then nonhierarchical mentoring, and then episodic lateral mentoring. (I threw that out as soon as it hit the page.) The point of this empathic nonhierarchical episodic lateral peer mentoring is to establish and intentionally use the power of our shared knowledge, experience, skills, values, and sisterhood to support each other on our way to a more just world.

The transition from cooperation to collaboration is not straightforward or guaranteed. It will happen (or not happen) differently for every group, and the essential element is trust. As essential as this is to a sisterhood community, *trust* cannot be definitively described.

I am reminded of Justice Potter Stewart's quote when the Supreme Court was struggling to define what was obscene and, therefore, not considered protected speech. He noted that he did not want to "attempt further" to define the kinds of things that would be considered obscene. "I know it when I see it," he said.[56]

---

55 Berat Özfidan, "The Difference Between Cooperation and Collaboration," Medium, April 13, 2019, medium.com/@beratzfidan/the-difference-between-cooperation-and-collaboration-4cda8868502f.

56 Peter Lattman, "The Origins of Justice Stewart's 'I Know It When I See It,'" The Wall Street Journal, September 27, 2007, www.wsj.com/articles/BL-LB-4558.

Though the courts certainly have to establish a standard to measure and gauge such things, we do not. We trust that we will all know when trust is established. We will struggle with it in the beginning. To some of us it comes easily; to others, not so much. In the pages ahead, I will describe examples of how to set out to establish this essential trust, but much like Justice Potter, you will know it when you feel it. Trust me on this. Trust yourselves to know.

COLLUDE

The sixth C-word sounds a bit ominous, as it connotes a negative or unlawful activity. Strictly speaking, to *collude* is to "cooperate in a secret or unlawful way in order to deceive or gain an advantage over others."[57] I thought perhaps the word *conspire* better captures what I mean: "working together to bring about a particular result, typically to someone's detriment."[58]

Truthfully, both of these words describe, in part, what I am talking about, but neither offers any possibility of a good outcome. There is a basic assumption that any "secret" cooperation is for some nefarious purpose or to someone else's detriment. I suppose if the powers that be like things just the way they are, any discussion of another way or a new accommodation would seem to be to the detriment of the status quo. But what if the purpose was noble and the desired outcome justice? Would these words still apply?

We can repurpose this word. Let us agree in the sisterhood that when we must *collude* for a common cause, we are indeed cooperating in a secret way in order to gain an advantage over the current system. The system cannot see us and is not thinking about us, and our efforts to date have yielded little progress, thus making collusion a rational and logical option.

---

57 Lexico Dictionary, s.v. "Collude," accessed October 31, 2021, www.lexico.com/en/definition/collude.

58 Lexico Dictionary, s.v. "Conspire," accessed October 31, 2021, www.lexico.com/en/definition/conspire.

This takes trust too. Everyone does not have to agree on a particular way to proceed, but they must agree that it is a worthy goal and that other attempts—those of this group of women or of those who have come before—have not yielded a result worthy of their efforts.

CODE PINK

My favorite example of a sisterhood colluding is a quite well-known story among nurses—the Code Pink story.[59]

In a small rural hospital, there was a long-standing problem of an enormously gifted surgeon berating, bullying, and occasionally flinging objects at nurses. There had been numerous complaints against this doctor to the director of nursing as well as to the hospital administration. The answer was always the same: "We will have a word with him."

Not only did this do no good, but it seemed to embolden this doctor, as he was well aware of what everyone knew: Nothing was going to happen to him. There would be no consequence for his actions. He was a singularly accomplished and sought-after specialist. The hospital and the region were very happy to have him, and his work enhanced the reputation of the hospital.

The sisterhood of nurses *connected* around this issue. They began to *collaborate* around possible solutions, discarding each one as something that had been tried, something they knew would not work, or something that might put one of them—or rather their jobs—in jeopardy. They *colluded* in secret to build a solution that would relieve them of their anxiety and fear of working with this doctor. And they arrived at Code Pink.

It was decided that whenever any of the nurses or nurse's aides were abused by this doctor, one of them would call a Code Pink, which would be whispered from nurse to nurse. Code Pink was the cue for all nurses not engaged in critical patient care at that moment to proceed to the site

---

59 Not to be confused with how many hospitals today use Code Pink to signal that someone is either impersonating a nurse or attempting to kidnap a baby. Josephine Ensign, "Re-Scripting Code Pink," Josephine Ensign, May 16, 2011, josephineensign.com/2011/05/16/re-scripting-code-pink/.

of the abuse and simply stand silently behind or next to their sister nurse.

As I tell this story, I enjoy thinking of myself in both places, thinking how magnificently supportive it must have felt for that single nurse and also how affirming and simply delicious it must have felt for her colleagues.

I do not know how this story ended. I imagine that the doctor kept up some sort of bad behavior but turned it down a few notches. I do know that when Code Pink first began, he complained to the director of nursing that when he was "correcting" a nurse, he was disturbed that they were summoning "witnesses." If I were writing the screenplay, I would have the director of nursing ask him something akin to "Perhaps all the nurses want the benefit of your instruction?"

This was a shared problem. The nurses were, as the definition states, cooperating in secret to gain an advantage, but unlike the definition, it was not to have advantage over others but to simply demand mutual respect.

Pinky Gloves

My entry for the best example of a world designed by men and for men, with women as an afterthought, is Pinky Gloves. Three men pitched this "innovation" on Germany's version of *Shark Tank*. It was a pink plastic glove to wear when removing tampons or pads with the added "benefit" of being able to turn it into a baggy sort of thing for disposal.[60]

The sisterhood of those who menstruate or have menstruated responded in an explosion on social media, tweeting and retweeting their disdain. The well-deserved critique of this product accused the founders of "mansplaining periods," solving a nonexistent problem (as if looking at or, heaven forbid, touching icky menstrual blood needed a remedy), adding more plastic to the waste stream, period shaming, and more.

---

60 Danielle Keiser, Milena Bacalja Perianes, and Marianne Liyayi, "A Tale of Two Pinky Gloves: A Bloody Shame Ends in a Remarkable Victory in Germany," Medium, April 20, 2021, madamithoughts.medium.com/a-tale-of-two-pinky-gloves-a-bloody-shame-ends-in-a-remarkable-victory-in-germany-6fd2eca98ef4.

Already *connected* by our common experience with menstruation, women could immediately *collaborate* and *collude*, albeit organically, by stating and repeating, sharing, and building on each other's opinions and reactions. Women quickly, effortlessly, and with all sorts of humor and creativity, formed a sisterhood community of pushback against Pinky Gloves.

By April 2021, the founders and the investor issued a tepid apology and removed the product from the market. They admitted that the "product and the communication with it was not well thought out." They went on to "apologise to everyone whose feelings and emotions have been hurt," noting that "we can understand why so many are upset about it."[61] They referred to this as a "mistake" and then congratulated themselves for bringing attention to the "taboo surrounding periods and to furthering the social discourse." And in their final tone-deaf communication, they stated that while they would listen to constructive criticism, they had been subject to hate speech, so "please remain objective with your justified criticism."[62]

As appalling as it is that this product even made it to the broadcast, even worse is that it got funded, particularly when compared with the general lack of investment in women-led companies. A pink plastic glove is hardly an innovation. Beyond the unlikelihood of getting funded, I cannot help myself from imagining the global firestorm that would ensue if three women were to "invent" a pocket penis wipe for those last few drops that do not shake off.

I hope the Pinky Gloves case is one that is taught in marketing classes. I like to imagine the teacher issuing an array of challenges to the class, including, "What might've been the very best response to the pushback?"

---

61 Sophie Foster, "Company Removes Pink Period Glove From Market After Backlash and 'Death Threats,'" Daily Star, April 21, 2021, www.dailystar.co.uk/real-life/company-removes-pink-period-glove-23953059.

62 "3 Guys Created a Pink Glove for Disposing Tampons. Give Us Strength," Today UK News, April 15, 2021, todayuknews.com/politics/3-guys-created-a-pink-glove-for-disposing-tampons-give-us-strength/.

Just imagine if the founders' response had been "What were we thinking, designing a product for women with no women on the team? No wonder we got it so wrong!"

Women could feel recognized and respected, and we could return respect to the team for offering up their gaffe as a teachable moment about the value—no, the necessity—of including women in the design of all consumer goods, particularly those intended exclusively for women.

And a sad and exasperating addendum to the above story? The actual Pinky Glove was sized to fit a man's hand. It was too large for the average woman's hand!

Think back to the Six Cs: *collide, communicate, connect, cooperate, collaborate,* and *collude*. Imagine what is possible when a sisterhood colludes! By its very definition, we are not alone. Collusion requires multiple ideas, strategies, and actions. We might collude in order to stand as witness to abuse or injustice, as in the Code Pink story, or to give a nudge to conference planners by not choosing sessions with a dreaded "manel" (the all-male expert panel). Or it might simply be a way for us to express a silent collective objection to a frustrating inequity—like the forms that still require us to indicate marital status! (For those forms that will not let one proceed until each question is answered, I sometimes check them all—single, married, divorced—as each has been true at one point in my life.)

When we stand together in silence or with volume, for a one-time objection or as part of a continuing movement, when we do any of these things for ourselves and each other, we change the world a little bit, sometimes imperceptibly, and our ordinary, good enough actions do in fact make something truly extraordinary.

CHAPTER 8

COMMON CHARACTERISTICS OF SISTER GROUPS

Consider the Six Cs the basic foundation of a group. But before you begin overtly forming or participating in a sister group, allow yourself to consider why this effort is important. Allow yourself to trust that the idea of a sister group is tacitly pre-agreed to because of women's current circumstances, and thus allow yourself to feel bold and entitled enough to propose it.

I still struggle to identify the key ingredient that brings women together in a sister group. It is a bit like Justice Potter stated about pornography, "I know it when I see it," but I can't perfectly describe it. It is some sort of restlessness. Some sort of awareness that we don't thrive in the system of the status quo. Some knowledge that this system is not rigged in our favor, a longing for something different, something that we cannot describe save in terms of knowing what we *don't* want.

This is all women. All women I know. All women I have known, and women yet to come—until the system changes. And though I do not suggest that we completely stop communicating, cooperating, and collaborating in our usual ways, I suggest that we prioritize doing it differently whenever we can—each day as individuals and whenever an opportunity presents itself for us to do it in a group.

In my personal sister group, the Seven Sisters, we set out to help each other find our next job, business, or cause. But we ended up discovering our own unique abilities, our own secret sauce, the things that came to us as naturally as breathing that we had long taken for granted.

I suspect it was the ease in using those particular skills and sensibilities that made us discount them. We have long been conditioned to work hard, identify our weaknesses and try to improve on them, and find a mentor to gift us with help along the way of our careers—only after we had proven ourselves worthy, of course. But when our individual special sauce—the things that others count on us for—was pointed out to us, we felt the shift. The tears that fell were definitely not tears of weakness, but tears of relief and release that recognition gave us.

Forever and always after that moment, we knew that we would never again have to prove to someone—to anyone—that we could do X or Y or Z. What we could do was in our bones and obvious to our colleagues. We could think of it as personal power and consider where we wanted to use it next, rather than something that would qualify us for a job.

The results were subtle but immediate. We got a glimpse of ourselves—our powerful selves—through the eyes of trusted others. Instead of thinking or saying, "I work well with people" or even "I'm good at building teams," we could now know and say to ourselves things like "I am highly skilled at bringing people together. I do this naturally and easily by being trustworthy and building trust in the group. This is important because it allows people to feel free to ask questions they might be reluctant to ask and to bring up new approaches or critique old ones; it builds morale; and it makes for a pleasant and effective workplace."

I submit that all women want this. As we become aware that our individual behavior will not change a system that is not rigged for our success, even the hint of an idea that there is an easier way that is joyous, delightful, and effective is interesting to all women.

Characteristics of the Group

Naturally, every sister group is very different. But there are some characteristics they have in common:

A Random Grouping

Earlier, I noted the importance of the random nature of the group. If we curate our group by choosing individuals with a certain characteristic or establishing criteria in order to be invited or included, we have already put an unintentional bias into our group. When I invite people to join me in something, I normally choose people who are like-minded or who I think might be interested. Instead, let us assume that all women are "interested"—all women have the key ingredient of wanting things to be different—and simply trust that a somewhat random group will benefit all of us.

When we think of gathering people, it is usually for a specific purpose—socializing, supporting, working. And though sister groups can do all of those things, the difference in this kind of group is that we establish and intentionally use our shared knowledge, experience, skills, and values—our power—for our individual and collective purpose.

Not a Friendship Group

Friendships may result from these connections, but they are a side benefit. For the group process to work, the members do not have to be friends.

Some of the most useful and actionable feedback I got from my initial sisterhood group was from the woman I liked the least. I was whining that "I don't know what I do. I am a generalist, an English major. I'm not an engineer like you and don't have an MBA pedigree or C-suite experience. Who's going to listen to me?" My at-the-time-disliked colleague sighed audibly.

I asked, "What?" She said she wasn't sure I wanted to hear what she had to say.

"No," I protested. "I can hear whatever you're thinking."

When she was finally convinced, she said, "You know, you've been saying that for almost as long as I've known you. That you do different things, and you don't really know what you do or what sort of work to look for. Frankly, I'm tired of hearing it. I'd love to have had the experience that you have. You have a ton of experience that translates into all sorts of possible jobs. Just start writing some proposals to places you'd like to work or consult. If they say no, ask them what they liked and what they didn't like, and go write another one! If you don't know how to write a proposal, ask one of us. Seriously, of all of us, you may well be the smartest, and you've certainly had the most varied background."

Ouch. I won't say that didn't smart, and I won't say that I immediately acted on it. But I will say that I heard it and I knew what it meant. It came from a trusted colleague, albeit one I didn't like, telling me the truth as she saw it. As hard as this was to hear, it was the thing I needed in order to dispel the myth I had created. The picture of action that she drew was the opposite of the lethargy and inertia I had been dragging around with me like flypaper on my shoe.

A few months later, that same colleague responded with generosity when I called to tell her I didn't know how to price my services and I could use some coaching on the script to introduce myself to a potential client. She made herself available, spent unhurried time with me on the phone as I took notes, and asked me to let her know how it went. I have called her many times since. I'm happy to report that we developed a lovely friendship, and she will absolutely recognize herself in these couple of paragraphs. Even when I'm not calling her with a question or to help problem-solve some reluctance I have, I call her up in my mind and ask myself, "What would she do?"

TRUST

One of the key ingredients to being a sister or participating in a sister group is trust. The most important things to trust are your own desires and intentions and to extend that by default to those in your midst. In fact, trust is the bedrock requirement for the group to work—a particular kind of trust that is freely given, freely received, and is reliable. Oh, that all our relationships would have this sort of trust, and I think they might if we began by first establishing trust rather than relationship as the goal.

We are all giving off cues that we are trustworthy, but from an early age we are taught that some people are trustworthy and others are not. We are conditioned that if we extend trust where it is not deserved, we will suffer the consequences.

Many of us are stingy with trust. I know I am.

But trust is as simple as it is tricky. It does not come easily for many of us, so it requires a bit of a leap. Take the leap. In the same way we can assume all women experience chronic fatigue and extraordinary-ism, we can also assume that our group participants, including ourselves, are worthy of trust. It is foundationally important that we put some words to it early in the group process—and then trust that it is happening.

Once while at an all-agency meeting in Washington, D.C., I was distracted and struggling with an ongoing family crisis back home. I'd shared the details with only a couple of my Sisters. During one of the sessions, I had gotten some sudden bad news from home and needed immediate space and privacy—to get out of the very public meeting venue. One of my Sisters saw this, said a few words to another, and then someone led me down some stairs and into a waiting cab to go back to the hotel. I assumed they had let our boss know. I recall that when I rejoined my colleagues later that day, the looks and smiles and pats on my shoulder assured me that all were glad to have me rejoining the day and, more importantly, that I wasn't going to have to make an explanation. My Sisters had somehow taken care of that. I don't know if the words "we've got you" were spoken, but it was clear to me that the Sisters indeed had me.

If this had been early in my history with the Seven Sisters, I would have been astonished. But because I had by now experienced the power of our sisterhood, their attention and action on my behalf was not surprising. It was a beautiful enactment of what we were and what we did for each other.

If you build a group from scratch, you may not have examples that signal trust, so it will be part of your initial communication and connection to speak affirmatively about it. You might say, "Trust is important for these connections to work well. What should we do in the event that any of us are uncomfortable with trust?" The conversation that follows that question will be all you need to take your next steps.

TRUTH-TELLING

Always tell the truth. It is important to give and receive authentic feedback. We cannot build trust if we give our group members well-meaning but inauthentic praise. It is important that we not undersell our value and power or represent ourselves in any sort of embellished or grandiose manner. Our goal here is to help each other, not to make each other feel good. If you have concerns about trust, you must raise them. If you worry that hearing the truth is scary for you, say it. Consider the sister group as a life lab—you get to say and do things you are not accustomed to saying and doing.

Once my kindergartner brought home a drawing for me. I loved it because he had made it for me. I wasn't quite sure what it was, so I said, "Thank you. It's beautiful." To which he said angrily, "No, it's not. I scribbled it, and it's not good." I was busted by a five-year-old. I didn't set out to lie to him, but because the relationship and his feelings were my first priority rather than his future art career, a seemingly innocuous untruth seemed an option. But now he had to wonder if I didn't know what beautiful was or if I was lying to him.

So it is with sisters. They will not benefit from inauthentic praise. And though we don't want to be either cavalier or aggressive with our feedback, it is more important that we are more truthful than tactful. Like my five-year-old child, people feel when we are not being authentic. The sad result of that is that it undermines their trust in us. They know we have said something we know not to be true; thus, our advice and our words are not reliable.

There are a number of steps and tips that are helpful for you to know, but more important is that you and your sister group find your own rules and rhythms by simply trusting each other and yourself to tell the truth—without exception.

THE GROUP HAS LEADERSHIP BUT NO DESIGNATED LEADER

To begin, there will be an inviter or a temporary host—the group spark. As the group forms, you may decide you need a facilitator. If so, be sure to rotate the role so that ownership of the group is fully shared. Remember to model "good enough," not extraordinary, when facilitating. In every group interaction, you have an opportunity to do things differently. Show up on Zoom in your pajamas with bed hair and no makeup—without apology. It is your brain and your being that powers the sisterhood, not your outward put-togetherness.

EVERYONE HAS PERMISSION TO USE THE GROUP FOR THEIR BLATANT SELF-INTEREST

This will be a work in progress for most and thus requires consistent reminders. There is no quid pro quo requirement to be a part of a group. The expectation is that your first concern will be how you can use the group to support you where you are or help you do or think something differently.

For example: "I need a résumé. Who can help me with that or suggest a resource?" Notice that the request is straightforward. There's no apology for not having a résumé already or for needing help, no explanation about your experience or lack of it, and most of all, no need to bargain. There is no need to say, "If someone can help me with X, I can help you with Y." It is simply assumed that if you ask for help or clarification or feedback, it will be given. No records are kept about who gets or gives the most help. It is irrelevant.

BEGIN WITH A COMMON AGREEMENT OR GOAL

This should be broadly stated with room for interpretation. The global reason for this book and for the interactions that it seeds is to establish and intentionally use the power of our shared knowledge, experience, skills, and values for our individual needs. State it informally and descriptively in your own language. For example, "We want to support every woman specifically and intentionally in a way that is easy and effective," or "We want to help each other in our transitions (new job, no job, downsizing, children leaving, baby coming)."

EXPECT THE GROUP TO BE TIME-LIMITED

The group is very likely to be time-limited, even if you intend for it to be ongoing. Be aware of this possibility and be sure to know it does not diminish the meaning or value in the least.

I loved our sister group. And as our jobs ended with the end of the administration, we all transitioned to the next chapters in our lives with varying timelines and degrees of ease. We had to work at staying in touch. We tried various ways and times to communicate—regular conference calls or Skype meetings (before Zoom and COVID and a time when people were accustomed to online conversations), rotating the facilitation of the meeting, and using a scoring tool to determine what was most important to us.

It happened slowly and uneventfully, but over a few months the logistics of connecting became increasingly difficult, and it became apparent that our initial expectation of consistent communication was unlikely.

We were sad about the gradual erosion of our connection. Wait, let me own this—*I* was sad. I understand now that our group was an amazing and transformative connection. It changed my life and the way I can now see my role in it. It served a sacred purpose, and it will not be replicated.

If I could have a do-over, I would want to be able to anticipate that regular communication would naturally come to an end. I would want to be even more affirmative about acknowledging the unique and profound importance of the group's power. And most of all, I would respect it by not trying to shape it into something it wasn't or by thinking we had failed somehow in that we did not keep it going. It served its purpose and bonded us in that experience. That sisterhood will sustain us whether we meet or not.

Now that I'm writing this, I want to reach back to the other six of the Seven Sisters and have this conversation I just described. I love the thought of this. No judgment, no apology, no regrets—just an "I want to be sure that you all know how my life was so positively transformed by the sisterhood we shared in our formal group and how I still love you all."

Since the original Seven Sisters, I have participated in a handful of such groups: two of them work-related (one lasting a few weeks, the other a few months), one a weekly neighborhood soup group (lasting a couple of years), and another a group of empty nesters missing our daughters (lasting a few hours). I have carried friendships out of each of those groups, but they came together, served their purpose, and dissolved with little fanfare—the latter without even an acknowledgment at the time.

We empty nesters collided and went immediately to collaborating and colluding as our level of trust was quickly and firmly established. Our almost tacit agreement was to be in touch with one another when we felt invisible to our daughters. The group is no longer, but the agreement remains.

CHAPTER 9

Commonly Held Goals

Just as every group is vastly different but all share some characteristics, so too do all groups hold some common aims. Most of these have to do with gaining the skills we've talked about—giving ourselves a break, extending empathy on the fly, telling the truth, being direct, etc. All of these skills require practice, and we practice with each other. As with gaining any skill, we will not be graceful or accomplished when we first begin to learn it.

Therefore, the overarching goal must be to give ourselves and each other a break—many breaks. Have compassion when your sister attempts to tell you the truth and it comes out a little brutally. Trust that her intention is good, and she is learning, and try to give her feedback that models a little more grace. Laugh whenever possible. Affirm each other for having the courage to try.

Keep the Relational Decks Clear

It is every group member's responsibility to speak up when something is amiss, whether it be some unspoken difficulty or some unfinished business. When the group has clarity of purpose and an agreement to tell the truth and build trust, any bumps, disagreements, or letdowns can be easily cleared as they happen or as soon as they are recognized. Everyone shares the responsibility for this. This is a work in progress as you all gain the skills, so give each other room to practice. Not doing this work will result in a stuck group and damaged trust.

Example: Mary defers her leadership turn as she's not good at moderating groups. Her sisters remind her that no one is an expert/everyone is an expert. Clumsy leadership is completely fine. If she would like feedback, she is invited to ask. If not, she can assume that the collective understands that group facilitation is not her strength, she's nervous about it, and yet she did it. The group gets to practice empathy, and Mary gets to practice group facilitation without fear of judgment.

Example: Joan is the only mother in the group with small children and notes that the meeting time does not work well for her, as she has to pay for additional daycare in order to attend. She offers possible solutions (remember, in her blatant self-interest): She can participate via Zoom, she can ask for the group to consider a different date, or she can suggest that everyone could Venmo her $5 for the additional childcare. If you winced at that last suggestion, good. It is exactly the sort of openness and self-interest that we want to be practicing. If suggesting reasonable compensation—"asking for money" as we might call it—feels uncomfortable, the sister group is exactly the place to try it out.

Example: Susie asks Marjorie if she changed her mind about gathering on Zoom since Marjorie missed a call she had agreed to attend and was late for this one. Susie is not trying to shame Marjorie; she is being direct and asking a question to get information.

AIM FOR FOCUSED INFORMALITY BY HAVING AS FEW RULES AS POSSIBLE

Whether you choose to meet in person, online, or a mixture of both, keep in mind that regularly scheduled meetings are not likely to work for everyone. As you begin, you may meet with some frequency to meet each member's needs and build your connection. But as you go along, you may switch up the frequency or move to an ad hoc style where any participants can call a meeting at any time and the group will respond as you have agreed.

Model and Practice a Very Brief Check-in

It is difficult to avoid the time it takes for everyone to report on how or what they are doing. Not everyone has to put their voice in the room. One strategy for brevity is to begin by asking how everyone is by a show of thumbs. Up means good; down means not so good; and to the side, meh. Then ask who wants some airtime to talk briefly about their thumb position. This is not the time to ask for help—that comes later in the meeting. This is just to share how life is going if you want to, to be seen.

Perhaps no one has a desire to say anything, or all or some want to say something. This could be the joy of a new client, a pregnancy, a new medication that is working, a decision to leave a job, frustration around a work or home situation, or the sadness of a loss. Sharing good news is as important as sharing hard times. Everything is welcome.

If the check-in gets distractingly long, say something. This is everybody's responsibility, but it may not be bothering everyone. If it is bothering you, say something.

Practice Empathy and Truth-Telling

As we will see in the next chapter, one of the great benefits of sister groups is the opportunity to practice new skills. And as we learned in Chapter 5, empathy is one of the most important. One commonly held goal among sister groups is to practice this with each other. But do not confuse this with sympathy. The point of true empathy is to let the person know that you see her and you understand what she is saying or experiencing, not that you are sympathetic or that you are necessarily joining her in what she is describing or feeling.

Example: If one of the sisters is angry about being fired from her job, one that she had professed to hate, resist the instinct to express sorrow about the job loss, to sympathize. When you are tempted to give knee-jerk comfort, false praise, or unwarranted positive feedback, remind yourself that this is not useful in a sister group. Asking her what type of job she might imagine not hating is the more empathic response.

This, too, takes a lot of practice. Give yourself and each other permission to be clumsy as you practice compassionate truth-telling. It is good to think ahead of time how you might want to word less-than-complimentary feedback. Humor works very well here.

Practice authenticity, or simply withhold statements that will not ring true for you.

Example: You don't have to say, "That's poorly written" but instead "That didn't really land for me" or "I don't really understand your point."

Or when a group member, a sister, doesn't follow through on a commitment, instead of "I thought you were going to do this," something more pointed might be called for in order for trust to be restored, such as: "You committed to do this, but I noticed you are not keeping your word. Has something changed?"

Example: With my five-year-old, instead of "That's beautiful," I could have said, "I like the colors in your drawing. Tell me about it."

TAKE ACTION EVERY DAY

The skills you practice together need constant development. Make daily action a goal of your group. Every day, quickly calibrate your mindset to remember that *all* women deserve empathy and that whenever you can, you will make some intentional expression of it. (I still have to do this calibration frequently, as *not* doing this was a multi-decade habit. So give yourself a break if it doesn't immediately feel natural.)

Next, make an overt gesture of empathy on the fly. Wherever you might collide with a woman and have an opportunity to communicate—whether verbally or nonverbally, with a few words, a roll of your eyes, a smile, or a shrug that says "I see you, I get it"—*do it*.

It is not complicated, nor is it easy. It is a new habit, and like most new approaches or mindsets or actions, it will feel awkward on the way to becoming a new way of being.

I recall having my right arm in a sling for a short time. It felt so foreign to offer my left hand in response to an expected handshake. I would always start to explain about my right hand being in the sling, which was obvious, of course. After a short time, I was quick to offer my left hand clumsily in a still-awkward handshake, but affirmatively, with a nod or smile that was always returned. It felt weird—until it didn't.

Once the habit is established, or nearly so, begin to imagine and then to believe that you can use this habit of empathy on the fly in a powerful way—with individuals and also in your sister group.

CHAPTER 10

How to Build a Sister Group

We have talked about the Six Cs and the magic of the power in groups. And we have looked at common characteristics, goals, and benefits of sister groups. Hopefully, you are hungry to experience this magic. Let us talk about the practicalities of building a group. Some of this will be familiar from Chapter 6 but is now in the format of an easy-to-follow guide:

Step 1: Colliding to Connecting

Someone has to be the spark! If you are reading this, *you are that spark*. You are the ignitor. There is plenty of fuel out there to burn and a near infinite number of sisters wanting to feel that warmth. But it will not happen without the spark. Someone has to communicate something to start the blaze, no matter how small. Remember that once you collide with two or more other women, you are already a group—albeit loose and random. Make the decision to move to informal but intentional. Feel free to refer to this book as your inspiration for wanting to leverage the wisdom and experience of the women in your midst.

There are three approaches that I almost always use in some form when I cross the boundary to connect with women I may know slightly or with whom I have just collided. You will eventually develop your own, but in the meantime, feel free to use mine.

1. "You know, _name_, our paths haven't crossed all that much, but you've always been someone in my periphery that I've wanted to get to know better."

2. "You know, _someone you know slightly or have worked with_, one of the things I've noticed about you is your _____ (integrity, sense of humor, ability to sum things up, irreverence, how you make everything beautiful and special even if it is just a sandwich, etc.), and I want to get to know you better."

3. And here are a couple of juicy ones—perhaps uncomfortable initially—that are just disarming enough to signal that this conversation is more than small talk; it is one of connection: "I admire the way you_____." Or, "I like how you said that." Or, "I appreciate how you _____, and I wanted to be sure to let you know that," and "Can you tell me, _name_, what you count on me for? What do you see as my unique ability?" I sometimes preface this one with: "When I get overwhelmed, I forget my own strengths."

STEP 2: COOPERATING TO COLLABORATING

The intention to collaborate is the turning point for a sister group. In the beginning, you need not have a specific project in mind. We didn't in my original sister group, other than seeking to give and receive support from women in our midst—an antidote to the isolation that comes with women's busy lives.

It may happen that you organically begin to collaborate, particularly if you are in frequent contact with one another. But it is more likely that it will be intentional. Here again, it needs a spark. It might be a current event that triggers a group response, moving toward action becoming a logical next step. Or the spark may, once again, be you or one of your sisters. It might sound something like this: "I have an interest in _topic_ (an idea, cause, job, or a burning question) and some time to devote to it.

Do any of you have half an hour in the next week to kick it around with me?"

Members – In my beloved first sister group, we collided as colleagues. We did not all like each other at first, and if I were to choose a group of women to bond with, this would not have been the group I would have curated. If left to me, I would most likely have chosen six women much like myself. But that sort of echo chamber would not have led to the transformative experience I had. My random grouping of likable and not-so-likable sisters was the absolute perfect group. How much I liked or didn't like them turned out to be completely irrelevant to our sisterhood.

Size – It must be at least three. There is something transformative about how we communicate when the third person is added to a conversation between two people. Some research indicates that groups become less effective with more than eight.[63]

STEP 3: CONTINUING TO CONCLUDING (Q & A)

Our original Seven Sisters group grew mostly organically without an obvious intention or strategy. The following are questions we Seven might've asked ourselves in the beginning, and your group will certainly benefit from thinking and talking affirmatively about them.

Think of them as possible shortcuts rather than prescriptions. For us Seven Sisters, the answers were obvious to us in retrospect. We had learned them as we went along or discovered we had known them all along.

Q: What builds trust?

A: Speaking affirmatively about the need for trust, truth-telling, keeping your agreements and holding others accountable for theirs, kindness, and humor.

---

[63] Capers suggests the optimal team size for productivity is 4.5. J. Richard Hackman, *Leading Teams: Setting the Stage for Great Performances* (Boston: Harvard Business Review Press, 2002); Capers Jones, *Applied Software Measurement: Assuring Productivity and Quality,* 2nd ed. (New York: McGraw-Hill Inc., 1996).

Q: How do you achieve consensus around a common goal?

A: If the group does not reach full consensus, speak to it. Note that you do not have consensus and ask whether that presents an unworkable problem. Get approval from all members to continue without consensus and ask what that would look like or choose a different focus.

Q: Do you ask for confidentiality?

A: This is a group preference but must be clear. Many of the things discussed or worked on will not require confidentiality, but others will (quitting a job, health problems, family problems, etc.). Be overt about what can be spoken of and what stays in the group.

Q: What is the role of the facilitator?

A: The rotating facilitator sets the agenda and the tone for the meeting and keeps it on track. Each person will do this differently—some, very informally; others, with more structure.

Q: What if you are not good at facilitation?

A: Perfect. This represents an opportunity to practice in a judgment-free zone to give and receive honest feedback, to accept good enough for yourself and each other, and a chance to build trust. Trust yourself; trust your sisters.

Q: What if I am not getting what I want?

A: Tell the group what you want and be specific if you are not getting it. Be a part of enabling what it is that you want. The biggest part of truth-telling is often giving voice to the unspoken complaint. Do not let a complaint be silent.

As for what you do not want, don't worry about it. It might be just what somebody else wants.

Q: What about the person who talks all the time?

A: Use truth-telling; give honest feedback with kindness and/or humor.

Q: How do you deal with conflict?

A: Conflicting opinions and perspectives are not a problem. They are additional information.

Q: What if somebody's feelings get hurt?

A: Great, again. First, if someone alerts the speaker or the group at large that her feelings have been hurt, good for her for saying it. It is a call for empathy.
In our group, we developed a convention of simply saying "ouch" if something landed in a way that was hurtful. I was that person more than a few times, and I recall one facilitator stopping to ask if I wanted to say more about the hurtful feedback. I honestly said, "No," adding, "I don't think so." She then asked, "Do you need a moment to catch up?" That was exactly what I needed!
I love thinking about how important this moment was for me and for the group. I did not need sympathy. I needed to hear the feedback. At the same time that my Sisters gave me the needed criticism, they responded with empathy to my "ouch." They didn't minimize it but instead made sure to offer me some airtime if I wanted it, or just enough space and time to catch my breath and come back to the present.

Q: How do you consciously practice empathy and truth-telling?

A: Clumsily and consistently with kindness and humor.

Q: How do you know when it is time to say goodbye, and what is the best way to do that?

A: This will be different for every group. The variables are numerous. If the group is focused on a task, completion of the task is a natural point to end the group or, at minimum, discuss both ending or continuing as options.

As the situation changes or as a task is completed or jobs and proximity come to an end, an overt and intentional discussion will be required about what is next, or whether anything is next. An affirmative discussion about endings ought to be a minimum.

The transition is likely to be messy, and the chances are strong that the group will not continue. Acknowledging the end of the group is as respectful as it is difficult. We missed that opportunity with the Seven Sisters.

Our Seven Sister group sort of fizzled out. Our jobs ended as the administration changed, and, though we had the intention to stay formally linked (which we did for a time), we were not able to keep the connection vibrant. We struggled with electronic communication in different time zones (this was pre-Zoom), some of us working, others of us not, and some of us fitting it in around family schedules. We intended to develop a workshop to present at a major conference or do some writing together, but, in retrospect, I believe we underestimated the weight of the transition and did not focus sufficiently on what that meant to the way we gathered and communicated.

We did not call a formal end, perhaps in part because we knew we did not want to end this extraordinary group. I certainly did not, and I believe my Sisters felt similarly. Once I experienced the power and comfort of this group, I could not imagine being without it. I understand now—better said, I trust now—that I can be part of creating this phenomenon with groups of women over and over, and I need not fear the ending.

That said, I suspect these endings might always be a little messy until we have had enough experience to know that this sort of sister connection remains available to us. My first sister group was so very special in that it was the first; it was where I learned the power of honest, empathic communication and interaction. And once learned, it could not be unlearned.

We Sisters remain connected, in great part because of our acknowledgment that our connection was transformative, and we bonded around that watershed moment. We are all interested in how each other is doing;

one or another of us will reach out for a specific purpose or event. When there is a hurricane or other disaster near one of us, the rest are in touch to be sure all is well. Each time I see one of their names in my inbox or hear one of their voices, I am uplifted and reminded of not just our connection but the power—personal and group—that we uncovered together. It remains a resource. One Sister recently suggested that we ought to get together for an "energy booster." I think she is on to something.

CHAPTER 11

Benefits of Sister Groups

The tangible benefits of your Sister group/mentor group are many and various. The most powerful one, in my experience and in that of the original Seven Sisters, is the transformative power of being recognized and recognizing others. To see and be seen. It is so cliché to say it this way, but I cannot overstate its impact. It is profound and yet difficult to properly describe.

The Sisters Speak

It was in the context of our group of Seven Sisters that many of us had our seminal experience of the power of empathy.

One Sister said: "It was a new [and] unknown feeling—being safe in a judgment-free zone."

Another noted: "I remember thinking, 'So this is what it feels like to be valued. This is what it feels like to not be judged. This is what it feels like to be appreciated for my work as well as the way I do it, my perspective.'"

One Sister explained that once she viscerally realized her own value, as reflected by the other Sisters, she would often ask herself: "How can I respect the truth of my value if I don't demand it beyond the Sister group? It made me realize that I deserved respect and recognition of my skills, experience, and value, and I didn't need to accept less."

The power of empathy is compelling as an interrupter to the E-Cycle™ of being *extraordinary*, becoming *exhausted*, seeking *empowerment* (which is actually just another to-do list to be better or more efficient) and further *encumbering* ourselves as we cycle back around to being chronically *extraordinary*. Once we learned from our Sisters, from each other, that we chronically are and deliver extraordinary, then we could add the empathic realization *no wonder* as we reached or approached exhaustion.

We learned that we cannot give true empathy until it has been given to us. Furthermore, once we have extended empathy to ourselves, we set ourselves on a path that reveals something new and different at every turn.

As one Sister noted: "Once you feel it, it can't be unfelt."

One Sister described the power of acceptance, forgiveness, and even humor that she had come to count on. "We do not immediately or always act affirmatively on our own behalf," she noted.

She added, "Each time . . . we say yes to something we didn't want to, act smaller than we really are, when we didn't speak up, or doubt ourselves professionally or personally, we can forgive ourselves, accept ourselves, and even laugh about it with our Sisters."

More from the Sisters

Each of us Seven Sisters learned how much and how often we had underestimated and minimized our own skills and abilities, and yet at the same time we could so easily see them in each other. Our agreements of truth and trust encouraged us to appreciate and value ourselves as we did each other.

> "I remember being in awe of everyone's strength and experience. You were all so good."

> "The breadth of our diverse experiences and capabilities was fascinating—the depth of each Sister in their areas of passion and expertise."

"One of the things that was important to me was . . . sharing with the Seven Sisters on the subject of the interconnection of our networks. We all are now 100% privy to each other's networks."

"You all had so much experience, deep and diverse. I was so impressed with everyone's accomplishments. And then I saw how you all thought of me and my experience just the same. I was impressive to you."

"Don't ever fret about your sister as your competition. By virtue of being a sister you have already won, whether you each know it then or not. Life happens in seasons, so be kind."

"What was reflected to me of me by my Sisters was my first experience of being recognized, truly recognized, [and] it made me realize that I deserved respect and recognition of my skills, experience, and value, and I didn't need to accept less."

Thinking back to the group, they added:

"My primary feeling as I think back is mostly gratitude. I wouldn't be where I am today [without the group]. I don't think I would have taken the difficult steps I took to get here were it not for the Sisters."

"I like how I learned to value myself. I keep my phone on silent and answer at my convenience. I am not afraid to say no if it doesn't work for me."

"If it isn't on the schedule, it doesn't exist for me. Someone else's poor planning is not my emergency."

"I schedule gym time, laugh time, and me time."

"I miss the organic banter that proximity enabled. I miss the sheer diversity of the brilliance each member brings."

"Truth-telling became our brand."

"Don't try to create impressions. 'No' to you and from you does not mean 'no' of you. In the same vein, 'yes' to you and from you does not mean 'yes' of you."

"Living for me now means [to] seek help when you need it, help how you can when asked, and if you can't be honest, make no assumptions about others."

AND FOR ME

When I heard each of my Sisters describe my strengths in their own particular words, I was overcome. I had no idea that the things they valued and counted on me for were visible, never mind important, supportive, and unique. They said things like:

"You are our mother spirit."

"You stand up for all of us."

"We feel strong when you are in the room."

"You don't let anyone mess with us."

I have always thought of myself as a bit of a rebel and as an extrovert more comfortable speaking than holding on to words. I often thought of both of these things as liabilities, that perhaps I should be a better listener and talk less. That maybe the odd, rebellious, or alternate way of doing something was not the best. Perhaps I should give more consideration to the traditional, the status quo. In my felt experience, these were not strengths and qualities that people appreciated and relied upon.

"You are our guru. Don't you know this about yourself?" one of my Sisters said. "When we start to discuss some concept or something that was published in the *Federal Register* that is new to us, we are all on a similar level with it. The second time we talk about it, you are the expert; you know the topic in a deep and meaningful way. Every time this happens. You do your magic research and condense things down to their essence. You explain it so it is easy to understand on its own, and it becomes clear how it fits in a context. We count on you to do this."

Yes, I do research topics that are new to me. I enjoy it, I am fast at it, and, apparently, I am good at it. I never thought of this as a strength because it comes easily to me. What I thought as simply making a basic summary or an analogy or example of how I understood the task or concept, others received as a primer or a study guide, and they counted on me for it.

I learned to trust myself and my strengths from my Sisters. Since then, it comes easier to me to list these things when asked to describe what I do or what a client can expect from me. I can easily say, "You can count on me for *all those things my sisters noted*."

I want to stop here to feel that feeling again. Tears still well up. Years later, it is still overwhelming to feel the generosity in their words, to know that the things I love and am good at are seen and valued in the world. I am uplifted to think that my sisters benefit from and even rely on my strengths. I am astonished by the flood of emotion I feel when seen, simply being recognized for who I am. It is profoundly moving to me to imagine the power of all of us doing this for—all of us.

SPECIFIC BENEFITS

As the group finds its form and the connection clicks into place, you can immediately feel the benefits of the give and take. Here are just a few ways you can use the group to your (and everyone else's) benefit:

Practice Skills and New Behaviors with Each Other

You can use your sister group to practice skills and new behaviors. You can do this organically as the opportunity arises or overtly ask for time to work on something specifically.

You can practice:

- intentional on-the-fly empathy
- asking for feedback
- giving feedback
- saying no
- receiving a compliment or giving one

In addition to practicing, do not forget to share examples of the above that you have experienced or created.

Ask for guidance (as specific as you need)
Example: "I don't know how much to charge for my consulting services. What do you recommend?"

I struggled with this problem when I started consulting. I had been in elected office and worked in government for much of my career, where my intellectual property (support, advice, and advocacy) was something I dispensed widely with no thought of how much it was worth. When I finally asked the question, "How much should I charge?" the answer was $300.

"A day?" I asked.

"No—an hour" was the reply.

Ask for a script if you do not know how to say something.
Example: Another Sister had a similar issue. Though she was comfortable with how much she charged, she found that she was giving a lot of her

time and advice away before establishing an agreement with a potential client. She did not know what to say to make her terms clear. She wanted to know very specifically what to say and how to say it.

The advice one of the group members gave her was to be overt about her "pay wall." Say something to the potential client like, "We can schedule a thirty-minute discussion at no charge so I understand your issue and you understand how I work. After that, my rate is $X an hour."

And if she forgot and slipped over her own boundary line?

The advice was to quickly say, "Oops, I forgot to put up my pay wall," or whatever phrase felt comfortable. The key was to have a phrase in mind and use it. The final advice the group offered was a reminder to give herself the grace to feel clumsy or awkward. This would be a new perspective and behavior, so she was to aim for good enough, not extraordinary.

Change your mindset

You can use your sister group to find a new way of thinking and being. To give yourself permission to use the group in your self-interest with comfort. To begin letting go of the need to be chronically extraordinary. To adopt a goal of good enough, adequate, or maybe adequate-plus in the majority of the things you do. Save your extraordinary work and approach for things that resonate with your passion, your spirit, and things that bring you pleasure, joy, and abundance. To feel the resonance of being in a sisterhood with truth-telling, trusted women.

Respite and Debriefing: Enjoyment

It is helpful to know how you want to benefit from the group going into it. If your group has respite and debriefing as its primary reasons for convening, even that can work as long as it is expressly discussed. Spend some time together communicating about what you want from one another. Then see how many positive results occur that you had not even imagined.

CHAPTER 12

NO MATTER WHAT

A QUESTIONNAIRE THAT WAS CIRCULATED AMONG APPROXIMATELY ninety women via an informal, nonscientific sampling technique revealed many similarities even across generational divides. What would become just over forty responses in a snowball sample began with me disseminating the questionnaire to a group of ten women of varying ages and geographies with a request that they pass along the link to up to five women of differing ages, occupations, and locations.

To the question "Do you feel supported by the women in your life?" just over a third of the respondents listed "sometimes" as their answer to the question, and just a bit under 10% said they were not supported at all by women.

It is considered countercultural for women to routinely and intentionally help each other. We have been conditioned and socialized to think that if we have found some level of success, it was a fluke. We are sometimes cajoled to think that we succeed because we "are not like most women" (or like the other *girls*, as I was "complimented"), as if this is some sort of praise. And, of course, many of us have swallowed the myth that there is not enough room in (fill in the blank with any traditional male role that has good pay and high status) for "our kind." If we somehow end up there, we ought to keep our head down and not encourage other women who might take our place.

Do not believe it. We can begin by rejecting the myth, the tacit message, that we succeed because we are special or lucky instead of the truth: that we deserve our success and there is plenty of room for women in all the places and jobs formally or informally "reserved" for men.

Recognizing each other's strengths, the things that come easily for us—noting them, acknowledging them, and using them in our own and each other's lives for our common best interest—points us toward a path to a new way of doing and being.

We do not have to spend one ounce of energy or moment of time justifying, convincing, explaining, or apologizing. Instead, we can ask and offer and ask. We can help and accept help. We can admit to exhaustion and boredom and the knowledge that we can be extraordinary in a sprint or a calculated choice, but we are not to expect it of ourselves and each other as the rule, only the occasional exception to the rule.

All women share in the gender disparity. All women, even if they do not see it or believe it, deserve the empathy of sisterhood. We are all blunted and blocked and bullied by a system that is not rigged for our success. Empathy—intentional empathy expressed out loud for ourselves and for each other—is contagious. Once experienced and practiced, both by giving and receiving, it is contagious. The potential of this sisterhood is so much more than my foremothers could have imagined and will reach into the next generation in ways we cannot foresee.

This is the magic that my Sisters and I unknowingly created. Now it is your turn to receive the benefits we did. How do we feel joy within the daily knowledge that we exist in a world that is not designed or amended for us to thrive?

Always Reach Out First

We reach out. We do not stop reaching up, but it becomes our second priority. Our first priority is to reach out to be a sister and to have a sisterhood so that we can co-create a more just world and enjoy it and each other along the way.

We begin with the knowledge that we all must be seen, recognized, and considered in order for us to experience equity and balance. On the way, we *all* deserve empathy. So, we model these behaviors and attitudes with one another for the rest of the world. Who better to see and understand the overt and covert baked-in gender bias and imbalance in the everyday life of a woman than a sister?

We default to empathy with our sisters. We cannot spend one moment wondering if a woman is deserving. Instead, we must teach ourselves and one another to default to the position that we all are deserving.

Sisterhood as a Hedge against Regret

Another way sisters help each other thrive is to keep one another rooted in the present while having an eagle eye on our personal priorities. This book was written at the end of a year of COVID-19 pandemic isolation. The lessons of that time slowly reveal themselves, and I am certain they will resonate for a long while.

I am most grateful for my discovery of how affirming "now" versus "later" is and how powerful it is to examine our usual defaults in order to be certain we are making conscious choices.

Like many of us, I had packed lots of things into *later*. The things and people in my usual cycle were not necessarily the things and people I thought about and yearned for the most during isolation. It was more the things I had hesitated to do and all the people I had intended to make deeper connections with that weighed on my mind the most, the things that would take just a bit of initiative—that's what I was most packing into *later:* calling my old college roommate, planting versus planning a garden, telling a new acquaintance I wanted to get to know her better, seeing live music, greeting the people in my neighborhood intentionally and personally, traveling, and, yes, writing this book. I am amused now as I think about how I teetered on the brink of having more room for to-dos in *now* than there might have been in *later*.

All the stuff we stick into *later* is fodder for regret. The things we mean to do and the connections we mean to make feel like a collection of intentions until they turn into some sort of sad repository for things we know we are unlikely to get to.

Sisterhood is a wonderful hedge against regret. In an article on her blog *homeculture*, Meg Conley asks that we think of ourselves *and* each other. Instead of our steady focus on "reaching up," we are invited to "reach out."[64] She invites us to *see* one another. When we are invisible, it is so easy to be swallowed up by the drudgery of doing, overdoing, and being chronically extraordinary, thinking that all that work is the solution to the too-much of our lives.

When our lives become a series of must dos and should dos that have little connection to what lifts us up, we feel very little but exhaustion. When we are seen and recognized, it is so much easier for us to remember who we are and what is important to us. When we reach out in sisterhood, we experience the mundane (and worse) in this context of recognition and sorority together. Our empathy for ourselves and others is enlightening. Over time it becomes joyous, delightful, and effective. It is powerful.

NOT ALL SISTERS NEED TO BE ACTIVISTS, BUT ALL ACTIVISTS NEED TO BE SISTERS—AND HAVE THEM

After decades of activism, I became aware of the hard edge I had developed and how the need for change loomed so large I could not find my way to comfort and joy with any kind of consistency. Though there are certainly big gains and policy goals and equal rights at stake for all of us, we need not—and honestly cannot—wait for justice before we live joyous and fulfilling lives. In the meantime, we can choose to practice overt and affirmative sisterhood each day.

Yes, all activists need to be sisters—and *have* sisters. Wherever we are in our own personal lives and timelines, we may not be able to fully participate as an activist, but we can applaud them, thank them, give them

---

64 Conley, "Motherhood in America Is a Multilevel Marketing Scheme."

data about women's lives/our lives, or simply feed them and encourage them to rest.

Not all sisters will be able or interested in raising the children of tomorrow. Still, they will be the sisters of those who are, remembering them and speaking of them and the need for childcare and healthcare in every policy discussion, understanding the value of their paid and unpaid work.

Not all sisters will be able to offer empathy to us or to themselves, but we can offer it to them—and to all—in their stead. The women I struggle to remember as my sisters are those on the furthest edges of my experience—the super-rich and successful (how dare they complain) and those who differ substantially from my political or religious worldview (I sometimes think they deserve what they get). But as we lean into a future of justice, denying *any* woman sisterhood serves no interest but the status quo.

AMY'S SISTERHOOD STORY

I began this book as an homage to my foremothers. I close it with a cherished non-hierarchical moment of lateral mentoring complete with intentional empathy and several of the Six Cs. I offer this very personal story as testament to the power and beauty in those too-clinical words. Consider this a sister gift from me and my mother, Amy.

I believe my mother, being one generation after my grandmothers, got a glimpse of the sisterhood, and it was my sacred privilege to have been the spark that illuminated the connection so that we could collaborate and collude as sisters for one brief exchange.

I had been planning a trip to Italy, but I was concerned about leaving my mother. She was not particularly ill, but at eighty-seven and in nursing care, we all knew our time together was not infinite, and I did not want to leave my sister with any additional burden while I was gone.

Six months before, Amy had been exercising, taking daily walks, doing her own laundry, having meals with fellow retired teachers, and ending each day at The Pub, where the coffee pot was always on right next to the never-ending plate of leftover sweets from the meals of the day. Then, as she deteriorated, she needed to move to nursing care at Renaissance Manor—a compromise for all of us, but a good enough, clean enough place with competent staff.

It was Mother's Day. "Our last one," I remember thinking. My sister, Susie, brought a picnic lunch with requisite cucumber sandwiches, slices of pear, and molasses cookies. The nurse wheeled Amy onto the patio to the "surprise" lunch and the "surprise" visit of both her girls. Susie was a weekly visitor, but I lived farther away and came only once or twice a month.

My mother turned to me and asked, "When are you leaving for Italy?"

I shot a look toward my sister, who shrugged, something like "*I know, I let it slip. She figured it out. I don't know.*"

"Yeah. I know the timing isn't great . . ." I said.

"I'm glad you're finally going to Italy," she said. And after a long pause, she added, "I guess I'll never get to see any of those places, will I?"

I answered, "I didn't know you wanted to travel, Mom."

One single tear trailed in a straight line down Amy's cheek to her jaw. She casually wiped it away and resumed talking. Susie left to get something. I shifted but held the silence.

"I guess I didn't know it, either. And it's too late now, isn't it?" my mother stated more than asked.

I took a breath. I so wanted to say, "Maybe not," but knew that that would not do. Sympathy would not have been the empathic response. In recent years, truth-telling had become my pact with my mother. It was our way to find some clear and special air to breathe above the loss, the dying, the friendly prattle, and the clinical taste and smell of it all.

"Yes, it is," I replied.

"Did you know I started college in pre-med?" Amy asked.

It took me a second to respond to her quick change of subject as I replied, "I didn't. I knew you liked science, but pre-med?"

"I wanted to be a doctor, but women, well . . . I got a low grade on my first organic chemistry test, and my professor told me I ought to change my major. I did—to biology."

"That's right, you taught high school science before we were born."

"A few weeks later, after I'd changed to biology, I learned that mine wasn't the lowest score in the class. But I was the only woman. Women weren't welcome in pre-med."

"Mom, really? Damn that makes me mad. What's his name?"

"Whose name?"

"That professor."

"Oh, I don't know, I don't remember his name. Why do you care?"

"I want to go piss on his grave."

"Lynn Bromley!" my mother said with feigned indignation. She looked down. "I wanted to be a scientist," she acknowledged softly.

"Mom, honestly, how could I not know this?" *What else is there that I don't know?* I thought to myself.

For those past six months or more, our mother had been apologizing to us—and we had been forgiving her—for mothering sins real and perceived. It was strange that she persisted with what had a whiff of guilt in it, or maybe it was regret.

She paused, a long pause, not as though she was trying to remember but more as if she was figuring out how to say it.

While I waited, I thought of my mother in college studying medicine, full of life, or "piss and vinegar," as she would call it.

I offered very quietly, "I'm thinking that being a wife and mother were not the top two things on your 'what I want to be when I grow up' list."

She looked up tentatively. "Is that bad?"

"No, Mom. They weren't the top two things on my list, either. I wouldn't want to draw a breath on an Earth that doesn't include my children. I know it's the same for you with Susie and I."

"Susie and me," Amy corrected.

"Right, with Susie and me. But I didn't set out to do this. It wasn't a plan. It wasn't my dream. Maybe not yours either."

Another tear, but this time it dropped onto her hand. Amy wiped it away with her other hand and looked up, startling me with a smile. Not one of those tight little oh-well resignations, but a big, toothy smile complete with wild eyes, engaged eyes, eyes that had an infinite capacity to take things in. Only now do I understand this as her response to being seen—to being recognized. I saw this unused, leftover capacity in my mother at the same moment she realized it was near expired.

"Lynn, you go to Italy."

"I will, Mom."

"No. I mean it, now. You go to Italy no matter what."

"I will."

My mother firmly grasped my arm just above my wrist and squeezed as she repeated, "No matter what."

* * *

We are on the way to justice, but it is not a requirement that we suffer along that way. We get to walk together in ways our foremothers could not. At the same time, we get to give joyous thanks for the courage it took for them to challenge norms and cross boundaries without a sisterhood. We get to thank them for the future they tried to imagine for us, and we get to repay them by widening this path for our sisters and our daughters so that challenging norms is never again a solo activity.

Sisters old and new and yet to be known are my nourishment, my sustenance in this world of inequity for women. I wish that my foremothers had had a sisterhood. I wish for my daughter and yours to have it, and for you, dear sisters. You are the cutting edge of sisterhood. You are the path walkers and the path makers, the signposts and the tour guides. You are my compass, and I am yours, so we can never stray far from the joy, delight, and effectiveness of walking together.

On the way to justice, let the new norm be sisterhood—no matter what.

ACKNOWLEDGMENTS

To all my sisters known and unknown, with immense gratitude, respect, and love for showing me the joy and abundance of a sisterhood and what it is to be a sister.

To my forever sister, Susie, and our shared history. For her love and humor and her annoying little-sister habits, like routinely beating me at cribbage.

To the other six of the original Seven Sisters—Ngozi, Jenn, Teri, Caitlin, Becky, and Yvonne. I am so blessed to have collided with you. Without your connection, your communication, your cooperation, your collaboration, your collusion, and your tender yet tough love, this book would never have been imagined.

To my all-star, all-woman, book-birthing team—Ashley, Kat, Mary Beth, Nina, Olivia, Courtney, Stephanie, and Jenn—for your skill, your wisdom, your belief in this work, and your sisterhood.

LYNN BROMLEY is a trusted, inspirational, and entertaining voice on public policy and gender justice. She is available to speak, present, or consult and may be contacted at www.innovationwomen.com or at info@lynnbromley.com.

ABOUT THE AUTHOR

LYNN BROMLEY is fascinated by change and inspired by small acts of courage. At different times in her career she has been a waitress, a teacher, a truck driver, a corporate manager, and a social worker. In 2000, she was elected to the Maine State Senate, where she served four terms and was later appointed to the Obama administration as the New England Small Business Advocate. Currently, she is the founder and principal at Fintech Advocate consulting. As a traveler, agitator, and champion of innovators, she is a global citizen and frequent visitor to kjæresten hennes in Oslo, Norway, but mostly lives in South Portland, Maine, near her two children and a great gang of sisters. She has been a woman throughout all her iterations and is a fresh voice on gender politics and justice.

Photo © Nina Fuller

BIBLIOGRAPHY

Apartment Guide. "Rent Report, October 2021: The State of the Rental Market." October 29, 2021. www.apartmentguide.com/blog/rent-report-october-2021-the-state-of-the-rental-market/.

Bateman, Nicole, and Martha Ross. "Why Has COVID-19 Been Especially Harmful for Working Women?" Brookings. October 14, 2020. www.brookings.edu/essay/why-has-covid-19-been-especially-harmful-for-working-women/.

BBC. "Only Men at Your Event? This Blog Will Shame You." May 27, 2015. www.bbc.com/news/blogs-trending-32789580.

Best, Alexis. "16 Alarming Sexual Harassment in the Workplace Statistics You Need to Know." Inspired eLearning. July 12, 2021. inspiredelearning.com/blog/sexual-harassment-in-the-workplace-statistics/.

Bittner, Ashley, and Brigette Lau. "Women-Led Startups Received Just 2.3% of VC Funding in 2020." Harvard Business Review, February 25, 2021. hbr.org/2021/02/women-led-startups-received-just-2-3-of-vc-funding-in-2020.

Blume-Kohout, Margaret E. "Understanding the Gender Gap in STEM Fields Entrepreneurship." Office of Advocacy. October 2014. advocacy.sba.gov/2014/10/01/understanding-the-gender-gap-in-stem-fields-entrepreneurship/.

Butler, Sandra S., and Luisa S. Deprez. "The Parents as Scholars Program: A Maine Success Story." *Maine Policy Review* 17, no. 1 (2008): 40–53. digitalcommons.library.umaine.edu/mpr/vol17/iss1/7.

Catalyst. "Historical Women CEOs of the Fortune Lists: 1972–2021 (List)." June 4, 2021. www.catalyst.org/research/historical-list-of-women-ceos-of-the-fortune-lists-1972-2021/.

Catalyst. "Women in the Workforce: United States (Quick Take)," October 14, 2020. www.catalyst.org/research/women-in-the-workforce-united-states/#easy-footnote-bottom-19-3975.

Conley, Meg. "Motherhood in America Is a Multilevel Marketing Scheme." Medium. December 7, 2020. gen.medium.com/motherhood-in-america-is-a-multilevel-marketing-scheme-f4ec1f536b04.

Cooper, David, Zane Mokhiber, and Ben Zipperer. "Raising the Federal Minimum Wage to $15 by 2025 Would Lift the Pay of 32 Million Workers: A Demographic Breakdown of Affected Workers and the Impact on Poverty, Wages, and Inequality." Economic Policy Institute. March 9, 2021. www.epi.org/publication/raising-the-federal-minimum-wage-to-15-by-2025-would-lift-the-pay-of-32-million-workers/.

Department of Economic and Social Affairs. *The World's Women 2015: Trends and Statistics* New York: United Nations, 2015. unstats.un.org/unsd/gender/downloads/worldswomen2015_report.pdf.

Ensign, Josephine. "Re-Scripting Code Pink." Josephine Ensign. May 16, 2011. josephineensign.com/2011/05/16/re-scripting-code-pink/.

Finney, Johanna. "Welfare Reform and Post-secondary Education: Research and Policy Update." *IWPR Welfare Reform Network News* 2, no. 1 (1998): 1–9.

Foster, Sophie. "Company Removes Pink Period Glove From Market After Backlash and 'Death Threats.'" Daily Star. April 21, 2021. www.dailystar.co.uk/real-life/company-removes-pink-period-glove-23953059.

Gender Avenger. "Home." Accessed December 13, 2021. www.genderavenger.com/.

Glassdoor. "3 in 5 Employees Did Not Negotiate Salary." Last modified August 2, 2020, www.glassdoor.com/blog/3-5-u-s-employees-negotiate-salary/.

Graffeo, Emily. "Companies with More Women in Management Have Outperformed Their More Male-Led Peers, According to Goldman Sachs." Markets Business Insider. November 11, 2020. markets.businessinsider.com/news/stocks/companies-women-management-leadership-stock-market-outpeformance-goldman-sachs-female-2020-11.

Great Business Schools. "35 Women-Owned Business Statistics You Need to Know in 2021." December 28, 2020. www.greatbusinessschools.org/women-owned-business-statistics/.

Gupta, Rudrani. "It Is Time Now To Recognise, Respect And Pay Women's Unpaid Labour." SheThePeople. March 22, 2021. www.shethepeople.tv/top-stories/opinion/pay-womens-unpaid-labour/.

Half, Robert. "What Is the Halo-Effect and How Can It Impact Interviews?." Robert Half. November 9, 2021. www.roberthalf.com.au/blog/employers/hiring-and-halo-effect-trap.

Hutt, Rosamond. "Do Women Work Longer Hours Than Men?." World Economic Forum, November 2, 2015. www.weforum.org/agenda/2015/11/do-women-work-longer-hours-than-men/.

Jones, Capers. *Applied Software Measurement: Assuring Productivity and Quality.* 2nd ed. New York: McGraw-Hill Inc., 1996.

Kay, Katty, and Claire Shipman. "The Confidence Gap." *The Atlantic.* April 15, 2014. www.theatlantic.com/magazine/archive/2014/05/the-confidence-gap/359815/.

Keiser, Danielle, Milena Bacalja Perianes, and Marianne Liyayi, "A Tale of Two Pinky Gloves: A Bloody Shame Ends in a Remarkable Victory in Germany." Medium, April 20, 2021. madamithoughts.medium.com/a-tale-of-two-pinky-gloves-a-bloody-shame-ends-in-a-remarkable-victory-in-germany-6fd2eca98ef4.

Kim, Anne. "Welfare Work Requirements Have to Go." Washington Monthly. April 17, 2021. washingtonmonthly.com/2021/04/17/welfare-work-requirements-have-to-go/.

Kuschel, Katherina, Kerstin Ettl, Cristina Díaz-Garcia, and Gry Agnete Alsos. "Stemming the Gender Gap in STEM Entrepreneurship—Insights into Women's Entrepreneurship in Science, Technology, Engineering and Mathematics," *International Entrepreneurship and Management Journal* 16 (2020): 1-15. doi.org/10.1007/s11365-020-00642-5.

Lattman, Peter. "The Origins of Justice Stewart's 'I Know It When I See It.'" The Wall Street Journal. September 27, 2007. www.wsj.com/articles/BL-LB-4558.

Lexico Dictionaries, s.v. "Collude." Accessed October 31, 2021. www.lexico.com/en/definition/collude.

Lexico Dictionaries, s.v. "Conspire." Accessed October 31, 2021. www.lexico.com/en/definition/conspire.

Madgavkar, Anu, Olivia White, Mekala Krishnan, Deepa Mahajan, and Xavier Azcue. "COVID-19 and Gender Equality: Countering the Regressive Effects." McKinsey Global Institute. July 15, 2020. www.mckinsey.com/featured-insights/future-of-work/covid-19-and-gender-equality-countering-the-regressive-effects.

Marçal, Katrine. *Who Cooked Adam Smith's Dinner?: A Story of Women and Economics.* Translated by Saskia Vogel. New York: Pegasus Books, 2016.

Martin, Emmie. "Here's How Much More Expensive Life Is for You Than It Was for Your Parents." CNBC. June 21, 2017. www.cnbc.com/2017/06/21/life-is-much-more-expensive-for-you-than-it-was-for-your-parents.html.

Martinez, Anthony, and Cheridan Christnacht. "Women Are Nearly Half of U.S. Workforce but Only 27% of STEM Workers." United States Census Bureau. January 26, 2021. www.census.gov/library/stories/2021/01/women-making-gains-in-stem-occupations-but-still-underrepresented.html.

McKinsey & Company. "Women in the Workplace 2021." October 14, 2020. www.mckinsey.com/featured-insights/spanersity-and-inclusion/women-in-the-workplace.

Miles, Ted. "On the Job: Women Launching a New Tradition." February 7, 2013, Southern Maine Technical College, South Portland, ME. Video, 27:06. archive.org/details/OnTheJobWomenLaunchingANewTradition.

Mohr, Tara Sophia. "Why Women Don't Apply for Jobs Unless They're 100% Qualified." Harvard Business Review. August 25, 2014. hbr.org/2014/08/why-women-dont-apply-for-jobs-unless-theyre-100-qualified.

Nam, Rafael. "'I Come Up Short Every Day': Couples Under Strain As Families Are Stuck At Home." NPR. November 12, 2020. www.npr.org/2020/11/12/929551120/i-come-up-short-every-day-couples-under-strain-as-pandemic-upends-life-at-home.

Özfidan, Berat. "The Difference Between Cooperation and Collaboration." Medium. April 13, 2019. medium.com/@beratzfidan/the-difference-between-cooperation-and-collaboration-4cda8868502f.

Peck, Emily. "The Gender Wage Gap Is Even Worse Than You Thought." HuffPost. November 28, 2018. www.huffpost.com/entry/gender-wage-gap_n_5bfd9d3fe4b0771fb6befd55.

Perez, Caroline Criado. *Invisible Women: Data Bias in a World Designed for Men*. New York: Abrams, 2019.

Reeves, Richard V., and Ember Smith. "The Male College Crisis Is Not Just in Enrollment, But Completion." Brookings. October 8, 2021. www.brookings.edu/blog/up-front/2021/10/08/the-male-college-crisis-is-not-just-in-enrollment-but-completion/.

Richard Hackman, J. *Leading Teams: Setting the Stage for Great Performances*. Boston: Harvard Business Review Press, 2002.

Sacks, Alexandra. "The Good Enough Mother." Medium. May 4, 2018. medium.com/@alexandrasacks/the-good-enough-mother-ab19fd-7dad06.

Sakowitz, Julia. "Uncovering the Gendered Dimensions of Job Hunting." The Clayman Institute for Gender Research. March 28, 2018. gender.stanford.edu/news-publications/gender-news/uncovering-gendered-dimensions-job-hunting.

Seguino, Stephanie. "Living on the Edge: Women Working and Providing for Families in the Maine Economy, 1979–1993." *Maine Policy Review* 17, no. 1 (1995): 43.

Slaughter, Anne-Marie. "Why Women Still Can't Have It All." The Atlantic. June 13, 2012. www.theatlantic.com/magazine/archive/2012/07/why-women-still-cant-have-it-all/309020/.

Today UK News. "3 Guys Created a Pink Glove for Disposing Tampons. Give Us Strength." April 15, 2021. todayuknews.com/politics/3-guys-created-a-pink-glove-for-disposing-tampons-give-us-strength/.

U.S. Bureau of Labor Statistics. "CPI Inflation Calculator." Accessed December 13, 2021. www.bls.gov/data/inflation_calculator.htm.

U.S. Department of Labor. "History of Federal Minimum Wage Rates Under the Fair Labor Standards Act, 1938 – 2009." Accessed December 13, 2021. www.dol.gov/agencies/whd/minimum-wage/history/chart.

U.S. Department of Labor. "State Minimum Wage Laws." Last modified September 30, 2021. www.dol.gov/agencies/whd/minimum-wage/state.

United States Census Bureau. "Census 2020 Quick Facts." April 1, 2020. www.census.gov/quickfacts/fact/table/US/SEX255219#SEX255219.

Zetlin, Minda. "54 percent of Women Report Workplace Harassment. How Is Your Company Responding?." Inc. March 2018. www.inc.com/magazine/201804/minda-zetlin/sexual-harassment-workplace-policy-metoo.html.